teach yourself®

retaining staff

edward peppitt

For over 60 years, more than 40 million people have learnt over 750 subjects the **teach yourself** way, with impressive results.

be where you want to be
with **teach yourself**

The publisher has used its best endeavours to ensure that the URLs for external websites referred to in this book are correct and active at the time of going to press. However, the publisher has no responsibility for the websites and can make no guarantee that a site will remain live or that the content is or will remain appropriate.

For UK order enquiries: please contact Bookpoint Ltd, 130 Milton Park, Abingdon, Oxon OX14 4SB. Telephone: +44 (0) 1235 827720. Fax: +44 (0) 1235 400454. Lines are open 09.00–18.00, Monday to Saturday, with a 24-hour message answering service. Details about our titles and how to order are available at www.teachyourself.co.uk

For USA order enquiries: please contact McGraw-Hill Customer Services, PO Box 545, Blacklick, OH 43004-0545, USA. Telephone: 1-800-722-4726. Fax: 1-614-755-5645.

For Canada order enquiries: please contact McGraw-Hill Ryerson Ltd, 300 Water St, Whitby, Ontario L1N 9B6, Canada. Telephone: 905 430 5000. Fax: 905 430 5020.

Long-renowned as the authoritative source for self-guided learning – with more than 30 million copies sold worldwide – the *Teach Yourself* series includes over 300 titles in the fields of languages, crafts, hobbies, business, computing and education.

British Library Cataloguing in Publication Data: a catalogue record for this title is available from The British Library.

Library of Congress Catalog Card Number: on file.

First published in UK 2004 by Hodder Headline, 338 Euston Road, London, NW1 3BH.

First published in US 2004 by Contemporary Books, a Division of The McGraw-Hill Companies, 1 Prudential Plaza, 130 East Randolph Street, Chicago, IL 60601 USA.

This edition published 2004.

Typeset by Transet Limited, Coventry, England.
Printed in Great Britain for Hodder & Stoughton Educational, a division of Hodder Headline, 338 Euston Road, London NW1 3BH by Cox & Wyman Ltd, Reading, Berkshire.

Hodder Headline's policy is to use papers that are natural, renewable and recyclable products and made from wood grown in sustainable forests. The logging and manufacturing processes are expected to conform to the environmental regulations of the country of origin.

Impression number 10 9 8 7 6 5 4 3 2 1
Year 2010 2009 2008 2007 2006 2005 2004

contents

part one

the facts about staff turnover and retention

introduction

In this chapter you will learn:

- **what it means to retain staff**
- **what retaining staff is all about**
- **the importance of key employees?**
- **how to use this book**

Employers are starting to take staff retention seriously. The make-up of the UK workforce has been changing steadily over the last twenty years. Nowadays we have record levels of employment, and employees can choose where and how to work. We are competing with other organizations, and other ways of making a living, to keep hold of our best employees. But what does this actually involve? And who are my key employees? This chapter introduces a subject that you simply must take seriously.

What is staff retention?

Employers are increasingly realizing the value of the people that make up their organizations. The issue of retaining staff has become very topical. As little as twenty years ago, employee loyalty was high, and few people would have considered leaving their job to go to work for a competitor. All that has changed.

These days it is the employee who takes responsibility for his or her career. If their current employer cannot offer a job as challenging, as motivating, as flexible or as well paid as they would like, then the quickest and most effective solution is to find an employer who can. For a number of reasons, staff loyalty has all but evaporated.

No wonder employers are looking at ways to look after their key employees. Staff retention is all about strategies that employers adopt to:

- identify key staff
- consider their differing needs and motivations
- introduce a package of measures, incentives, motivators and programmes to encourage them to stay.

No employer is looking for total retention. In most cases, this would be as serious a problem as total turnover. The skill is to allow a manageable level of staff turnover, which will bring fresh blood into the organization, while working hard to retain the key employees who will make a difference and deliver the business results you demand.

This book will help you to identify your key employees, and devise strategies that will greatly improve your chances of keeping them in your organization.

Who are your key employees?

Throughout this book, we talk repeatedly about the need to 'retain *key* employees'. But who are your key employees, and what makes them stand out?

Key employees

Key employees are employees who are important to you, and whom you would not wish to lose to a competitor. Examples include:

Experts in a particular field

For example, a software development company may have a programming expert who is always able to devise creative solutions to complex programming problems. He would be a key employee to the software development company, and they would not want to lose him to a competitor at any cost.

Specialist knowledge or skills

These employees may not be experts, but you have provided them with training and development which has resulted in them acquiring specialist knowledge or skills that give you a competitive advantage. They are key employees.

Good contacts

These are staff who have excellent personal contacts that are relevant to your organization. They seem to know who in the industry might help, whatever the issue may be. Their source of contacts is invaluable to you, and you would not want it to fall into the hands of a competitor.

Good people managers

Perhaps you have one particular team or department that always seems to outperform the others? If so, take a look at the person leading the team or department. He or she is a key employee. She seems to be able to motivate and encourage her team members better than her colleagues.

Long-standing staff

Do you have some members of staff who have been with your organization for a long time? Some of these people seem to mirror precisely the culture and work ethic of the organization. They know every policy and procedure, and how a particular problem was solved in years gone by. They need not be very senior in order to qualify as key employees. What is important is their knowledge of the organization, and the experience invested in them. They are especially valuable during periods of organizational change.

Graduate trainees

Yours may be an organization that runs a fast-track career programme for new and recent graduates. If so, then these graduate trainees should be considered among your key employees. You are investing heavily in their training and development, and this investment would be wasted if they left to work for a rival organization.

Key posts

As well as key employees, your organization may have one or more 'key posts'. These are positions which really need to be filled all the time. The performance of the business would suffer if these posts were left vacant for any length of time. Two examples of key posts include:

Payroll administration or book-keeper

If there was no one in position to administer the payment of salaries to your staff, then what effect would this have on the rest of your staff?

Retail manager

In a retail environment, managers have to be very 'hands on'. They often handle all the everyday procedures that keep the retail business functioning. You would not want this position to remain vacant for very long if the current jobholder left.

Some organizations are so concerned about key posts, and their importance to the business, that they devise succession plans to make sure that someone is ready to take up the post at a moment's notice if the person doing the job leaves.

Having considered key employees, and key posts, take a look at the staff that you employ:

- Who is currently working in a key post? How likely are they to leave in the foreseeable future?
- Who are your key employees?

It is sometimes worth writing out a list of the people who you think are most able to help your organization reach its business objectives. There are all sorts of games you could play:

1 If you could only keep two of your employees, who would they be?
2 If you were only allowed one manager, which one would you keep?
3 If you were forced to make redundancies, which positions are least able to influence the business objectives?

The answers to some of these questions should help you to identify exactly who your key employees are.

How to use this book

Teach Yourself Retaining Staff looks at all of the main strategies that organizations use to keep their key staff working with them. The book is divided into four main parts:

Part one: The facts about staff turnover and retention (Chapters 1–4)

This section looks at the way the job market has changed over the last twenty years, and the effect it has had on staff turnover and retention. It summarizes the principal external factors that influence retention, over which you will have little control. This section of the book considers the reasons staff give for leaving organizations, and the reasons that some employees stay. It offers simple methods to measure the level of turnover and retention in your organization, and suggests straightforward methodologies for comparing your results with your competitors and other organizations in the same business sector.

Part two: Recruitment, training and development (Chapters 5–9)

Many organizations suffer poor staff retention results that are caused by recruiting the wrong candidates in the first place. This section of the book provides a concise, no-nonsense summary of how to get recruitment right first time, every time. This section also looks at the critical role that training and development plays in motivating and retaining staff.

Part three: Money, motivation and benefits (Chapters 10–13)

Most employers believe that salary is the biggest issue that affects motivation and retention. Pay them more, they would argue, and they will stay. If only it was that simple. This section of the book looks at the overall salary and benefits package that you offer to your employees. It considers the reasons why you must design a flexible, retention package for each employee. Everyone has different needs and desires, and these must be satisfied by the package that you offer. What role do bonuses and commissions play? Why do some bonuses result in demotivated staff? When should you consider offering shares and share options in your company? How can you motivate your staff? This section answers all these questions and more.

Part four: Retention costs and effects (Chapters 14–17)

What does it cost to introduce programmes to retain your staff? How much will you save on recruitment, as well as on training and development? This section of the book looks at the practical issue of the costs involved. It also looks at ways to put retention strategies into practice. Where will you start? Why are so many people talking about the need to create a work/life balance? How should you plan to retain all the different types of staff that you employ? You will find all the answers in this section of the book.

02 external factors

In this chapter you will learn:

- **how external factors can contribute towards staff turnover and retention**
- **how demographic changes are altering the make-up and profile of the UK workforce**
- **about the effect that skills shortages have on recruitment and retention**

No matter how seriously you resolve to take the issue of retaining your best staff, there are many external factors over which you have little or no control. The state of the economy, the job market, and unemployment levels, will all influence the rise and fall of staff turnover. This chapter assesses the external factors involved, and helps you to establish the extent to which these are contributing towards your retention problems.

The job market and how it has changed

Perhaps twenty or thirty years ago, the concept of a 'job for life' was still a reality. The loyalty and trust that existed between employer and employee meant that leaving to work for a new employer was comparatively rare. You may know several people who have worked for the same employer for most of their working life, without even considering to look for alternative employment. Like a marriage, a job with a reputable employer was not something you walked away from lightly.

So what has changed over the last twenty years? With regard to the job market, the answer to this question is just about everything. With increasing local and global competition, organizations have had to change radically the way they operate. Mergers and acquisitions have become daily events, even involving the most apparently stable and established companies we know. Organizations have downsized and restructured, some several times, as competitive pressures have increased. Organizations have reduced costs, and outsourced many of the functions that formerly they conducted internally. Of course, many of these changes have been at the expense of the staff that had served them, and over time the loyalty that staff show to their employer has eroded.

In the 21st century it is the employee, rather than the employer, who takes responsibility for career development. People are ever more ambitious. If career progression is unlikely to come quickly from your current employer, then the obvious solution is to look for alternative employment.

Market research analysts Mintel published a study of changing working patterns amongst the British workforce in August 2003. Amongst their findings, Mintel discovered that:

- Ten million people have switched jobs during the last two years.

- One in ten workers aged 25–34 admitted having four different employers in the last five years.
- More than half of workers aged 55–64 have had only one employer throughout their entire career.

Mintel believe that changing jobs frequently is regarded as a fast way to boost career prospects. As an employer, you may not have any control over the way that the UK workforce is made up. However, if employees are changing jobs to boost career prospects, you need to consider some steps that you might take. Think about:

1 the prospects that you are able to offer your key employees
2 ensuring that these prospects are well publicized and known to your key employees
3 establishing formal career paths through your organization.

The issue of career prospects and progression is considered in some detail in Chapter 13.

The economy

In times of low unemployment, people have a much wider choice about where to work, and who to work for. So when unemployment is low, employers have to work particularly hard to retain their key staff. At the time of writing (October 2003), UK unemployment is at its lowest level for 28 years. There are plenty of employment opportunities open to people, and so staff turnover rates across all sectors are likely to be higher than average. Employers also have to work harder than ever to recruit the right staff in the first place when unemployment levels are so low. If you have been recruiting for new staff recently you may have experienced a lower than expected number of applications. When unemployment is low, you must have a strategy in place to recruit the right people, and retain the best staff that you have. If you don't look after them, then someone else will.

High unemployment can also affect staff turnover rates. Staff are much more likely to remain in their posts, whether they want to leave or not. Employers may have staff whose productivity has dipped, and who are clearly unhappy, but who are nevertheless unable to find alternative employment. High levels of unemployment often lead to lower staff turnover rates, which is good, but they also mean that staff who are dissatisfied remain in their posts, fearful that they might not find alternative employment easily.

Demographics

The age profile of the working population is changing all the time. Did you know, for example, that there will be 1.4 million fewer 16–24-year-olds in the labour force by 2006? Or that there will be 2.3 million more 35–54-year-olds by the same time? By then, one in six employees will be a woman with a child under the age of 16.

More school leavers are going into further education than ever before. There are new government initiatives to encourage men and women to retire at 70 rather than 65. Changes like these affect the overall composition of the workforce, and inevitably, your staff turnover and retention rates. For example, if you have traditionally recruited a number of school leavers each year, you may find that it is getting harder to recruit and retain suitable candidates.

Lower birth rates, and higher numbers of school leavers going into further education, have resulted in fewer young people entering the labour market than, say, twenty years ago. We have a higher proportion of older, adult workers. If you want to keep them, you need to think about the issues that concern them, and consider offering part-time positions, flexible working hours, family-friendly policies and so on. The issues of flexibility and identifying the needs of certain types of employee are covered in detail in Chapters 16 and 17.

It is not just the way that the workforce is made up that has changed. As individuals, there are countless other roles, responsibilities and cares that we have nowadays:

1 More of us own homes than ever before.
2 More of us have responsibility for the care of an elderly relative.
3 There are more single-parent families.
4 There are more working mothers.

And these are just a few examples. With all these changes, no wonder it is becoming so important to offer more flexible employment, including the following features:

- flexible terms
- flexible hours
- part-time work
- job shares
- term-time work
- seasonal work.

If your staff turnover rates are rising, you need to consider whether you are offering sufficiently flexible terms for today's workforce. If you are not, then you might be losing staff to a competitor who is. See Chapters 16 and 17 for some steps you can take.

Skills shortages

Skills shortages exist in certain industries periodically. For example, during the late 1990s, computer programming staff were in short supply, and often sold themselves to the highest bidder. If an organization employed a competent programmer, they did everything they could to keep them. HR Managers knew that if a programmer resigned, it would be a costly and time-consuming exercise to replace them. For certain programming jobs, they might not be able to replace them at all. Of course, once the dot.com bubble burst, the situation changed, and there is currently a ready supply of employees with good computer programming experience.

Skills shortages such as these are commonplace. They can be caused by new and emerging technologies, as in the computing sector, but they can also exist in traditional sectors and industries. In 2003, for example, the UK has a well-publicized shortage of nurses, engineers and plumbers.

Skills shortages also occur on a regional basis. There have been government initiatives for almost twenty years that offer incentives to companies and organizations moving to certain regions in the UK where unemployment is high, and in particular where traditional industries, such as mining and steel, have collapsed. Many organizations that have moved to these areas have had to invest heavily in training and developing their workforces.

Competition can also create skills shortages. If two or more competitive organizations are based in the same region, between them they may quickly absorb all of the appropriately skilled local population. In extreme cases, the reverse may be true. In Reading, in the UK, for example, you will find Microsoft and Oracle, the two largest computing companies in the world, operating from the same industrial site. As a result, however, they attract candidates from all over Europe, who know that their skills are likely to be needed in Reading.

Gender balance

Recent research from *Labour Market Trends* predicted that the working population would rise by 1.5 million by early 2006. We have already considered that the number of workers in the 16–24 age group is on the decline. In fact, 73 per cent of this predicted rise in the workforce is female.

The percentage of women in employment has risen steadily every year since 1984. Today, almost 70 per cent of women aged between 16 and 59 are employed in one way or another. Back in 1984, the figure was just 54 per cent. And it is still rising. By contrast, the percentage of working age men in employment has remained fairly constant over the same period, with the exception of the severe recession in the early 1990s.

The *Labour Market Trends* update of October 2003, published by the Office of National Statistics, revealed that there has been a substantial increase in the proportion of women returning to work after childbirth in recent years. In 1979, just 24 per cent of women went back to work within a year of having a baby. In 1996, this figure had risen to 67 per cent. If you are interested in reading the *Labour Market Trends* updates in full, you can download them from the Office of National Statistics website. Go to **www.statistics.gov.uk.**

Work/life balance

Today, around six million people have some sort of flexible working arrangement, which includes:

- flexitime
- job sharing
- term-time working
- annualized hours.

In fact, around 27 per cent of women, and 18 per cent of men, are employed in some sort of flexible way. The number of people working flexibly, and the variety of flexible working schemes, are both on the increase. The issue of flexible working patterns is considered in detail in Chapter 16.

Checklist

✓ Are you experiencing a greater than expected staff turnover?
✓ Do you consider that external factors might be to blame?
✓ Are the skills you require in short supply?
✓ Are there a lot of vacancies for similar positions elsewhere?
✓ Are unemployment rates particularly low?
✓ Have you always recruited from school leavers, or another sector of the workforce that is in decline?
✓ Could your location be contributing to your retention problem?
✓ Are you offering sufficiently flexible working options to your workforce?

In this chapter you will learn:

- **the reasons staff give for leaving organizations**
- **the reasons they give for staying**
- **what job applicants are looking for from employers**

Do you know the reasons why staff leave your organization? Have you ever asked them? It is important to question why staff leave voluntarily because it is only by understanding the causes that you can hope to take action to prevent others from leaving. Furthermore, the reasons employees cite for staying with an organization are often unexpected. Actively retaining staff is about more than just avoiding the factors that lead employees to leave. This chapter examines the reasons employees give for leaving organizations, the reasons why they stay, and what new employees are looking for in an organization.

When staff leave voluntarily

It is common for employers to believe that voluntary resignations are all but unavoidable. Employees tend to take employers by surprise, and voluntary resignations are often the least predictable type of staff turnover. However, employees resign for all sorts of reasons and you need to understand these reasons in order to take some control.

Take a look back at some of the occasions when employees resigned voluntarily from your organization. Do you understand the reasons that led to the resignations? Did you ask each employee why they were leaving? What reasons did they give? With hindsight, did the employees you asked give you the genuine reasons?

Larger organizations tend to collect data about the reasons employees give for leaving. Whilst this data can be useful, it is not always revealing. For example, it is common for an employee to offer a simple reason rather than go into detail about the underlying cause. The employee may not feel comfortable having to justify the decision that they have made. Employees may believe that if they voiced their real concerns, it might affect the outcome of any reference that you provide. An employee may feel unable to criticize the organization, or may just be keen to leave the organization on good terms and without fuss. Perhaps an employee was bullied or felt discriminated against? For all sorts of reasons, therefore, the employee may be unwilling or unable to voice the concerns that led to their resignation.

Nevertheless, canvassing the opinions of employees leaving can at least help you to understand the decision-making process that employees make. Many organizations conduct 'exit interviews' or issue 'exit questionnaires' to gather data about why staff leave.

Exit interviews

An exit interview is an internal interview designed to establish the reasons why an employee wishes to leave the organization. An exit interview is designed to establish:

- why the employee joined your organization in the first place
- what the best aspects were of working for the organization
- what the worst aspects were of working for the organization
- where the employee is going
- what type of organization the employee has joined
- the main reason the employee has decided to leave
- whether there is anything that the organization could do to encourage the employee to stay
- any other comments the employee has regarding their resignation.

Exit interviews are not intended to dissuade the employee from leaving. Rather, they are designed to establish the cause of the resignation, and whether there is an underlying problem that needs to be addressed. Is there a particular manager or colleague who contributed towards the resignation? Is pay the contributory factor? Does the organization offer sufficiently challenging roles? Is the lack of career progression an issue?

So, turning to your organization, ask yourself whether holding exit interviews would help you to establish why you are losing staff? If you do decide to conduct exit interviews in your organization, you should bear the following points in mind:

- They should be conducted by someone independent, preferably by a personnel or human resources expert.
- They should not be conducted by the employee's line manager under any circumstances.
- They should be treated with confidentiality at all times.
- They are often more productive if they are held away from the employee's workplace.
- They are best held as soon after the employee resigns as possible.
- You should always treat the employee with good grace. You should wish them luck and thank them for the work they have done for you (even if it is through gritted teeth!).

EXIT INTERVIEW

Name

Job title

Department/team

Length of service

Gender: Male/Female

Why did you join the organization initially?

Were your expectations met?

What were the best features of working for the organization?

What were the worst features?

What are the reasons that led to your resignation?
(Tick any that apply.)

- Pay ☐
- Conditions ☐
- Lack of promotion/career development ☐
- Poor training and development ☐
- Working hours flexibility ☐
- Workload/stress ☐
- Not enough challenge ☐
- Better job offer ☐
- Work environment ☐
- Relationship with manager/supervisor ☐
- Difficulty travelling to/from work ☐
- Domestic reasons ☐
- Other (please state)

What was the most important reason for leaving?

What might have encouraged you to stay, if anything?

Any other comments?

sample exit interview/questionnaire

If you are unable to hold an exit interview, you could ask employees who leave your organization to complete a questionnaire about some of the reasons why they are leaving. Whether you use a questionnaire or conduct an interview, remember that an employee will not always be entirely honest about all of the reasons why they plan to leave.

You may wish to refer to the exit questionnaire template on pages 18–19. You can use it to create your own questionnaire, or to provide the basis of the questions you might ask an employee at an exit interview.

If you notice that employees often give the same reasons for leaving, you may be able to anticipate problems that arise and take action beforehand. If pay is always the issue, then perhaps you need to review your remuneration policies. However, do not set too much store by what a single employee says. A poor exit interview may be the result of a single, disgruntled employee. Most organizations have one from time to time. You should not start worrying until you identify a trend emerging from a number of employees who have resigned.

When you analyse the exit interviews or questionnaires, make sure that you compare similar types of employee. Do part-timers give the same reasons for leaving as full-timers? Are younger employees giving the same reasons as older ones? Do male and female employees voice the same concerns?

The reasons staff give for leaving

Recruitment and selection

It stands to reason that if an organization has a poorly devised recruitment and selection strategy, then it is likely to appoint inappropriate and unqualified staff who will not thrive in their roles. Organizations with a thorough and well-planned recruitment and selection policy tend to suffer significantly lower staff turnover rates.

See Chapter 5 for practical help with recruitment and selection procedures.

Company policies and practices

There are a number of factors relating to the organization's policies and practices that might contribute towards a staff resignation. Perhaps the employee does not share your organization's values or culture. Maybe you have been through a number of changes recently that have affected the employee. If you are a small organization, then perhaps you are unable to match the rates of pay and benefits that the employee is looking for. If you have been through a merger or acquisition recently, then this may have unsettled the employee. If yours is a larger organization, then perhaps the employee feels that you have overlooked them for promotion or development? Company practices, whether significant or trivial, all contribute towards the way your employees feel about their work.

Training and development

Insufficient training or development is often cited as a contributory factor when an employee looks for another job. If an organization does not have a proper induction programme in place, the feeling of dissatisfaction can start as soon as the employee joins. Interestingly, employees are equally frustrated by irrelevant or unnecessary training, so training and development is an important factor in staff turnover rates. See Chapter 6 for ways to introduce an effective induction programme into your organization. See Chapters 7–9 for advice and help concerning effective training and development.

Job satisfaction

This is another common reason cited for leaving an organization. Employees may state that they felt undervalued, that their efforts went unnoticed, or that they received little or no feedback about their performance. An appraisal system is designed to provide two-way evaluation and feedback for both employer and employee, and organizations with a structured appraisal system in place tend to suffer lower staff turnover rates. See Chapter 9 for practical guidance about introducing an appraisal system, that will encourage employees to understand the role and contribution that they make to the organization.

There is another symptom related to job satisfaction. Employees may believe that their job offers too few opportunities. They do not feel stretched. They may voice this belief by saying something like they 'need a new challenge'. You may already know of staff who are not sufficiently challenged, yet you are unable to offer them a suitably challenging role. However, the feedback and appraisal systems that you should have in place ought to identify under-challenged employees long before the issue becomes a resignation one. You should be able to recognize employees who need to be stretched, and have measures in place to anticipate their needs.

Job satisfaction, or the lack of it, can take many forms. Employees leave for all sorts of job-related issues:

- insufficient responsibility
- lack of job security
- too little control of tasks
- schedules and deadlines too demanding
- too many tasks
- tasks too repetitive
- lack of variety
- too long working hours
- few opportunities to use skills.

Employers need to be aware of the skills that their employees have, and be prepared to make use of them in order to reduce the levels of boredom in their jobs. Remember that giving employees more interesting tasks to do does not necessarily mean that you need to give a greater quantity of work to do. There is no point in giving more interesting, varied work on the one hand, whilst adding to stress loads and pressure with the other. See Chapter 13 for help with issues concerning job content and job satisfaction.

Promotion

It is very hard to offer balanced promotion opportunities for employees. In smaller organizations, there might not be sufficient opportunity for an employee to progress as quickly as they would like. The employee may have to resign and work for a different organization in order to continue their career progression.

In larger organizations, employees might feel that they have been overlooked for promotion, and so have to leave in order to achieve the recognition they feel they deserve. They may see a colleague promoted ahead of them, and feel that it is unfair.

Increasingly, the emphasis for career progression is placed on the employee, rather than the employer, which has led to a rise in the number of workers switching employer on a regular basis.

The appraisal process, together with the appropriate use of personal development plans, can help to maintain control over the career and promotion opportunities that an organization offers. In any event, an organization should consider carefully the impact that promoting an employee is likely to have on their colleagues, department, team members, and on the organization as a whole.

One of the immediate ways to make an impact regarding your promotion policy is to ensure that all promotion in your organization is based on merit and performance alone.

See Chapter 8 for ways that your appraisal process can help to identify the employees ready for promotion, as well as the employees who need specific training and development to grow further in your organization. Chapter 8 also considers how to give employees regular feedback on their performance.

Stress

There is stress in every job, and stress is the highest cause of staff absence and illness in the workplace today. Since stress is often cited as the reason why staff leave organizations, is there anything you can do about it?

- Are you and your colleagues doing anything to prevent or reduce stress in your organization?
- Are you aware of members of staff who are under particular pressure at the moment? Is this pressure justified?
- Would you recognize the signs of stress? (Poor sleeping; short temper; easily upset; argumentative; lack of enthusiasm; anxiety and worrying; headaches and stomach aches.)
- Do you set realistic deadlines and targets?
- Are your staff appropriately trained in time and project management techniques?

Remuneration

There is no denying that money is a key reason why staff leave to work for another organization. The job may be very similar, but if another company is prepared to pay more than you are, then some employees are bound to be tempted. However, it is not as crucial an issue as many employers believe. Money is rarely the only reason why an employee leaves an organization (which is why it is almost never a good idea to encourage an employee who has resigned to stay by offering more money).

Often it is the *package*, rather than the *salary*, that is valued by the employee. Two companies may offer a similar salary, but one may position the salary within a broader, more appealing package, such as:

- season ticket loan
- flexible working hours
- generous holiday allowance
- contributory pension scheme
- healthcare provision.

Increasingly employees are looking for these, and other benefits, when they are looking for long-term employment.

Ask yourself the following questions:

- Do you know how your salaries compare with the packages offered by your competitors?
- Is your remuneration policy fair?
- Is it based on performance?

The answers to these questions, and others, may hold the key to retaining your key staff effectively.

It is worth stating that although pay is regarded as an important issue, and one which can cause an employee to stay or go, it is rarely the critical issue influencing staff retention. In most organizations, those who leave and those who stay are equally likely to complain about pay.

See Chapters 10 and 11 for practical help to address issues relating to money, perks and benefits.

Management

Many employees blame their resignation on their managers or supervisors. One reason for this is that it is common for employees to be promoted to management or supervision level, without proper management or leadership training being provided. Some managers are poor communicators, whilst others are poor at motivating their staff. Whatever the symptom, there are many poor managers in the workforce today.

Are you aware of teams or departments that are poorly managed in your organization? Do employees complain of poor communication? Have relationships between managers and employees led to staff resignations in the past? Have any exit interviews highlighted relationship problems as a contributory factor?

Any of the following might lead an employee to consider looking for alternative employment:

- lack of management
- little or no motivation
- insufficient supervision
- poor feedback
- lack of direction
- poor communication
- unapproachable managers.

Outside work

We all need to remind ourselves that we have a life outside the office. People often talk about trying to create a work/life balance, and employees might well consider an alternative job in order to achieve this. Perhaps an employee has a young family, and wants to spend more time with them? Maybe an employee has neglected a partner by working long hours and weekends in the pursuit of unreachable targets? Do you have staff who are on the road, and spend long periods of time in hotels and away from home?

Situations like these work for some employees, and not for others. You need to respect that people's situations change. Living out of a suitcase may have been fine for a single employee, living on their own. Once married, they are bound to have entirely different needs.

Increasingly there is a need to be flexible, and to try to look at each employee's case individually. What can you offer to support an employee who wants more time at home? What about someone who wants to go back to college? To work fewer hours? To work at different times? Chapter 16 looks at ways to work more flexibly.

Of all of the factors listed here as reasons why employees leave, the two most important are:

1 job satisfaction

2 management and supervision.

Contrary to popular belief, money, perks and benefits, whilst extremely important, are further down the list of employee priorities.

Interviewing the employees who stay

There is no reason to stop at conducting exit interviews with employees who resign. After all, your mission is to reduce unwanted staff turnover, and retain your best and most productive members of staff. So why not interview them as well?

- How are they feeling about their jobs?
- Are they satisfied?
- Are they motivated?
- Do they feel they are being challenged?
- Are they planning to change jobs in the foreseeable future?
- Where do they see themselves in two years' time?

All these are questions that should be asked during the course of an effective appraisal or performance review. However, if you are concerned about staff turnover, and about retaining certain employees in particular, then there is every reason to interview these staff at other times as well. If these employees are essential to the success of the organization in the short term, then you should consider getting answers to these questions as soon as possible. If you do not already have an appraisal system in place, then turn to Chapter 8 straight away to learn about the benefits that appraisals bring to an organization. In the meantime, consider having a chat, or even an interview, with the employees that will make a difference to you, if only you could be certain that they will stay.

What factors keep staff with an organization?

Research has shown that most senior managers and directors believe that the single reason why employees stay with an organization concerns their salary package. If you want to retain a member of staff, they would say, the solution is to offer them an increase in their salary package, in the form of:

- increase in salary
- new bonus and incentive payments
- additional employee benefits, such as pension scheme or healthcare
- a new or better company car.

However, whilst important, the salary package alone is not the factor that employees regard as the main reason for staying with their company or organization. The main reason relates simply to how much they enjoy their job. If, as an employer, you can provide *job satisfaction* to your key employees, then they are highly likely to stay. You will find a guide to the measures you can take to ensure job satisfaction in Chapter 13. If you can provide a job which is satisfying, as well as an attractive salary package, then you will be very well placed to retain your key employees for several years. Any other dissatisfaction that an employee may feel is likely to be disregarded if these main two factors are favourable.

Nevertheless, every one of your employees is different. Each will have roles and responsibilities that must be considered, and which result in different motivators in the workplace. In Chapters 10 and 11, we consider the various benefits that different employees will find attractive. Here, though, is a brief summary of some of the major factors that might influence your key employees to stay:

Job satisfaction

This is universal. Job satisfaction is the factor most likely to retain the services of a key employee.

Salary and benefits

Most employees will not leave an organization because of pay on its own. However, certain types of employee will be more influenced than others. Graduate employees may be looking to climb quickly up through the organization, and may expect an appropriate salary package to rise accordingly. To them, the salary and benefits offered may provide the most important influence on retention. Similarly, an employee with a young family may have to leave an organization on salary grounds, if they are not earning sufficient money to cover their extra costs.

Job security

Younger employees may not consider job security too important. For older employees, especially in poor economic conditions, job security could encourage them to stay with an organization indefinitely.

Flexible working and the work/life balance

This is becoming increasingly important. You can find out how to establish a flexible working policy in Chapter 16.

Training and development

Again, this is almost universal. Many employees complain about the lack of training and development to perform their role effectively. If you establish a systematic training and development programme that links individual employees to company objectives and goals, you will have an important element of your employee retention strategy in place. Chapters 7–9 consider how to do this.

Career development

Most employees need to see what their future with your organization might look like. Do you have guided career paths in place in your organization? Chapter 13 considers career development in more depth.

What new employees look for

We have seen that a poor salary may not be the sole reason an employee resigns. The same cannot be said when attracting new staff to your organization. A candidate applying for a job will not have experienced the job satisfaction that accompanies the role. They have not witnessed your structured training and development programme. For them, the salary package that you offer may be the single most important factor.

When looking for a new job, applicants have a shortlist of needs/wants that they will look to satisfy, including:

- attractive salary and benefits package
- job prospects and career progression
- well-known company?
- job location
- job security.

If you are recruiting for new staff in the foreseeable future, you should think carefully about the steps you will take. The staff turnover rates of many companies are influenced by poor recruiting choices. If you appoint the wrong person, they are likely to leave the organization within a relatively short period.

Look at Chapter 5 for guidance about introducing recruitment measures that increase your chances of making the right choice of candidate every time.

Checklist

✓ Do you know the reasons why your staff leave?
✓ Do you conduct exit interviews or use exit questionnaires?
✓ Are you recruiting the right staff?
✓ Is training and development an issue?
✓ Are you providing sufficiently challenging roles with job satisfaction and opportunities for career progression?
✓ Is pay a contributory factor?
✓ Are your managers providing effective leadership?
✓ Have you thought about the reasons why your retained staff stay with your organization?

04 measuring staff turnover and retention

In this chapter you will learn:

- **how to measure rates of staff turnover and retention in your organization**
- **how to use other measurement methods to analyse your retention performance**
- **how to spot trends, blips and anomalies in your staff turnover figures**

Do you believe that you have a staff retention problem in your organization? Do you know how your staff retention rates compare with similar organizations in the same sector? Do you know how many staff have left over the last 12 months, and what percentage of your workforce this represents? This chapter will help you to assess whether or not you have a staff turnover problem, and broadly where that problem lies.

Rates of turnover

There is a mathematical formula you can use to calculate the rate of annual staff turnover in your organization as a whole, or in just a team or department within it:

$$\frac{\text{number of staff leaving over 12-month period}}{\text{average number of staff employed over the same period}} \times 100$$

For example:

number of staff who left organization in 2003 = 14
average number of staff organization employed during 2003 = 75
Rate of turnover = $\frac{14}{75} \times 100 = 18.7\%$

The average number of staff employed can be calculated crudely by adding together the total number of staff at the beginning and end of the year, and dividing by two.

If yours is a larger organization, you may find that establishing the wastage rate for the entire organization is not particularly useful. For example, it will not take into account that various teams or departments may have differing rates of employee wastage. Neither will it account for the variation between staff who left voluntarily, and those who have been asked to leave. Nor will the formula account for any difference between staff who retired, and those who left to work for another organization.

However, if you perform the calculation for the entire organization, and then for the individual departments, you can assess quickly which teams or departments face particular staff wastage problems. Once you have identified the departments who have higher than average wastage rates, you can then probe further to establish whether this is caused by:

- the nature of the work that the team or department performs
- the age or experience of the staff that the department employs
- a specific issue to do with the management or supervision of the team or department
- some other issue.

When performing the calculation, you may decide to exclude dismissals, redundancies and other involuntary wastage. After all, you are concerned with improving levels of staff retention, so you may legitimately conclude that involuntary wastage can be regarded separately.

In addition to analysing retention rates for individual teams or departments, you may wish to look separately at other key factors:

1. If you broke down your employees by age group, and then performed the formula for each group, you could quickly establish how age influences wastage rates in your organization. Research has shown that rates of wastage should decrease with age.
2. How about length of service? It is generally acknowledged that the longer the employee stays in an organization, the less likely they are to leave. Is this true of your organization?
3. What about pay? If you divided your employees up by salary band, you could establish the extent to which pay and benefits affect staff turnover. Are lower paid staff more likely to leave then higher paid staff?
4. Hours worked? You could run the formula for full-time workers, and then again for part-time workers. Are your turnover rates higher for full-time workers, or lower?

You may know of other factors that you think might be influencing your ability to keep hold of staff. Can you express them in such a way that you can use the formula to test your assumptions? By using the mathematical formula, you should be able to identify some trends or factors that influence retention and wastage rates in your organization.

If you use this formula regularly, you should start to identify certain trends. But remember the limitations of looking at figures in isolation. Compare your statistical findings about turnover rates with what employees who left said at their exit interviews (see Chapter 3).

Rates of retention

By focusing on turnover rates, you are analysing the number and type of people who leave your organization. It can be just as illuminating to undertake similar analysis about the people who stay.

- How many staff have been with you for ten years or more?
- How many staff have been with you for five years or more?
- How many staff have been with you for two years or more?

For each case:

- Are they younger or older staff?
- Are they part-time or full-time workers?
- Are they predominantly male or female?
- Are they senior or junior staff?
- Do they have any other characteristics?
- Do they work for particular teams or departments?

The formula used to analyse retention rates is the same as before, except that this time you use the numbers staying, rather than the numbers leaving:

$$\frac{\text{number of staff staying over 12-month period}}{\text{average number of staff employed over the same period}} \times 100$$

For example:
number of staff who stayed with organization in 2003 = 61
average number of staff organization employed during 2003 = 75

$$\text{rate of turnover} = \frac{61}{75} \times 100 = 81.3\%$$

As with staff turnover rates, a calculation looking at the organization as a whole may not be particularly useful. You should measure retention by analysing groups of staff who have been with the organization for different periods, for example:

- Up to 12 months
- 12 months–2 years
- 2 years–5 years
- 5 years–10 years
- 10+ years.

Whilst the results will vary between organizations, you should be able to ascertain a time period beyond which an employee is likely to stay for a considerable period. You are likely to establish that the longer your employees stay with you, the less likely they are to leave. For example, take a look at the fictitious case study below:

Case study: Balloons4U Ltd

Period of employment	Retention
Up to 12 months	34%
12 months–2 years	42%
2 years–5 years	70%
5 years–10 years	85%
10+ years	96%

This company finds it extremely challenging to retain new staff, and staff who have been employed for less than two years. However, the retention rates improve dramatically once an employee has been with the company for two or more years. This analysis could be used to predict approximate retention rates in future years, given the make-up of staff and length of service.

Other measurement methods

So far, we have considered statistical methods for measuring retention and turnover. In Chapter 3, we also looked at how exit interviews can hep to identify the reasons why staff leave, so that you are ready to spot trends. There are a number of other ways you can measure factors relating to staff retention:

Absenteeism

Do you monitor rates of staff absenteeism at work? Do you suffer particularly high rates of absenteeism? High rates of absenteeism can be a symptom of stress in the workplace, and this in turn can contribute to higher rates of staff turnover.

Competitor comparisons

In some industries, it may be possible to compare one organization's retention rates with another. Could you do that? Consider your main competitor. Do you know, or could you find out, how many staff left over the last 12 months? Do you know, or could you find out, their total workforce size? If you can, you may be able to make a broad comparison between your organization, and your competitor's, with regard to staff retention. If their results are different from yours, what might be the cause? Do they have a younger or older workforce? Is their workforce predominantly male or female? Do they offer a different pay and rewards structure from yours? The answer to these questions may help you to establish whether you have a staff retention problem, as well as what the cause might be.

Benchmarking

If you or your organization is a member of a professional body, society or institute, you may be able to get from them average staff retention and turnover figures for companies and organizations in your business sector. These will help you to establish whether your staff turnover is above or below average for the sector.

Exit interviews

We have already seen in Chapter 3 how conducting exit interviews can greatly increase your understanding of why staff leave your organization. By looking at a group of exit interview summaries, or questionnaires, you may be able to break down leavers into one of the following categories:

- employees who retired
- employees who left for personal reasons which the organization could not influence (e.g. getting married, and moving to a new area to be with partner)
- employees who left to work for another organization
- employees who left dissatisfied with the organization and their term of employment
- employees who left for other reasons that the organization might have been able to influence.

Having segregated departing or departed employees into one of these broad categories, you should be able to include in any statistical analysis only those employees who left for reasons that the organization might have been able to influence. After all, you are unlikely to be able to offer terms that will retain an employee who is moving to live abroad. However, you may be able to offer beneficial terms to an employee who might otherwise leave to seek a more challenging position elsewhere.

Staff records

Staff records contain valuable data which can help you to identify where you are most vulnerable in turnover and retention terms. It is very useful to compile a staff audit periodically, which will assess your workforce in terms of:

- age
- gender
- length of service
- nature of role
- full-time/part-time
- seniority of position
- pay and rewards structure
- working hours
- distance travelling to and from work.

This audit, used in conjunction with both statistical retention measurements and exit interviews, can help you to spot where you are most vulnerable.

Specific questionnaires and surveys

If other measurement methods highlight particular areas of concern, you may wish to use questionnaires or surveys to investigate further. For example, suppose that a number of exit interviews have attributed stress as a major reason for leaving the organization. An examination of staff records has highlighted that there are at least twenty more employees undertaking similar roles. You will need to establish quickly and effectively whether the other twenty employees are feeling the pressures of the role, and whether this stress is likely to cause them to leave the organization. In this example, you could use a survey or questionnaire that asks employees about:

- the levels of perceived stress that accompany the role
- how well each member of staff feels they are coping with the pressure
- what employees are doing to handle the pressures
- what the organization could do to alleviate the problem
- how likely employees are to leave the organization as a result of the pressures involved.

Questionnaires and surveys could be undertaken confidentially, or even anonymously, in order the be sure that employees are open and honest with their comments and answers.

High retention can be dangerous

It may not be immediately obvious that a very high rate of retention may not necessarily be a good thing. There are some negative consequences that may arise as a result of a consistently low staff turnover rate:

- fewer new staff are being recruited, who might otherwise have new ideas and a new perspective that would benefit the organization
- good staff may be held up for promotion because there are too few opportunities that the organization can offer.

The skill is always to strike a balance between retaining the staff who can help your organization to achieve its business objectives, and allowing a rate of staff turnover that enables you to bring fresh blood in, and also promote the rising stars.

Blips and anomalies

It is important to exercise caution when interpreting the results of any of the measurement methods. The figures themselves may hide the real issues behind them, or lead you to believe that the problem is far more serious than it really is. Examples include:

- The organization's overall turnover rates are high, but this is because turnover rates are exceptionally high for the most junior roles involving repetitive tasks. For most other roles in the organization, turnover rates are below average.
- A staff survey indicates that stress levels are very high for employees in certain roles. You may conclude that you need to act quickly, and that you will lose staff in high numbers unless you do so. In fact, this perceived risk may not be as serious as you think. The way the survey was undertaken may have led staff to answer certain questions in a particular way. Remember also that a degree of pressure is often considered desirable to maintain levels of challenge and motivation.
- Turnover rates may be high as a result of an organizational change. This may result in a higher than expected number of resignations in the short term, but turnover levels usually return to normal after a short period.
- If your organization has had to make staff redundant, and these redundancies are included within the statistical analysis, it may look as though retention rates have plummeted. You should make sure that any analysis of retention includes only those employees who left your organization voluntarily.

Time bombs

Just occasionally, an organization may find itself facing an exceptionally high level of turnover, as the result of an initiative or scheme introduced several years before:

Case study

When CTT Group plc bought a small market research company called Sky Blue Thinking Ltd, it wanted to ensure that as many staff as possible were retained during and after the acquisition. As a result, individual share options, bonuses and incentives were offered to the key employees. However, most of the share options and bonuses were timed to mature at roughly the same time. So four years after the acquisition, the Managing Director, the Sales Manager, the Research Analysts and the Senior Marketers, all cashed in their share options and left the company. All in the space of six months!

It may seem like common sense, but if you are planning to introduce share options, rewards or bonuses to your employees, you must ensure that they do not all mature at the same time.

What next?

By now, you should be able to measure rates of turnover and retention across departments, teams, types of employee, or even the whole organization. In other words, you should now know whether or not your organization has a problem retaining staff. The challenge now is to identify what steps you can take to tackle the problem.

Checklist

- ✓ Could you express your staff turnover in percentage terms?
- ✓ Could you express your staff retention in percentage terms?
- ✓ How does the rate compare with previous years/periods?
- ✓ Have you looked at how turnover rates differ for younger or older staff? For staff who have been with you for longer? For men and women? For full-time and part-time staff?
- ✓ Is your organization particularly vulnerable in certain ways? For example, do you tend to lose most staff who have been with you less than 12 months?

- ✓ Does your analysis help you to identify some of the causes of your staff turnover?
- ✓ Have you considered the significance of other factors, like absenteeism?
- ✓ Do you know how your retention results compare with your competitors?
- ✓ Do you know how your performance compares with other organizations in your business sector?
- ✓ Have you included only voluntary resignations in your calculations?

part two

recruitment, training and development

05 recruitment and selection

In this chapter you will learn:

- **the importance of robust recruitment procedures**
- **how to advertise, shortlist, interview and select in order to recruit the right candidate for you**
- **the link between recruitment and retention**

In most organizations, staff turnover is higher in new and recently appointed staff. It tends to be harder to retain the new recruits than staff who have been with an organization for some time. This chapter considers why this might be the case, and considers why an organization's retention strategy should begin with recruitment and selection.

Measuring retention in new recruits

In Chapter 4, we looked at a simple formula you can use to measure rates of staff turnover. You can use the formula to compare turnover rates of staff who have been with your organization for less than a year, with those who have been with you for three or more years. You will almost certainly discover, if you did not know already, that you have higher turnover rates for staff who are new or recently appointed. So what is the cause, and what can you do about it?

The problem may well lie with your recruitment and selection procedures. In simple terms, you may just have recruited the wrong people in the first place. Virtually every organization would admit to having recruited unsuitable people from time to time. Poor recruitment can happen for a number of reasons:

- The skills required for the job were scarce, and so there were few candidates to choose from.
- The candidate selected seemed to fit what the organization was looking for, but then did not work well with the rest of the team.
- The candidate started off well, but got bored quickly and found another job.
- The candidate claimed that he had been misled about the true nature of the job.
- The candidate chosen was overqualified.
- The candidate chosen was underqualified.
- The candidate did not fit the culture of the organization.

If your organization has a robust and effective recruitment and selection process in place, then these scenarios may not sound familiar. However, if you suspect that your recruitment system may be to blame, you may find the following short guide to recruitment and selection useful.

Do you need to recruit?

When a member of staff resigns, you may feel tempted simply to recruit someone who has similar skills and experience to perform the same role as the outgoing job holder. However you should look at a staff resignation as an opportunity to appraise both the role to be filled, and the person best suited to it. The outgoing job holder's role may have developed over time in line with that person's skills and abilities, rather than in line with the needs of the organization. So take the time to consider:

- Could the role be filled by someone else in the organization?
- What skills and experience are required to fill the role?
- How has the role developed over time?
- How central is the role to the business objectives of the organization?

The answers to some of these questions may lead you to conclude that there is no need to recruit anyone after all. You might be able to reorganize an existing team or department. You may be able to outsource part or all of the role. Perhaps the role is more suited to a part-time position? Maybe there are other staff who are looking for additional responsibility, who might take on all or part of the role?

So when faced with a staff resignation, you need to look at the situation objectively, and seek answers to the following three questions:

1 Do I actually need to recruit?
2 What role do I need to recruit for?
3 What sort of person am I looking for?

Analysing the job

So you have confirmed that you need to recruit. The next step is to be sure about exactly what the job entails:

- What skills and knowledge are required for the role?
- What experience are you looking for in your recruit?
- What authority or responsibility does the role carry?
- What prospects does the position have?

Once you can answer these questions you will be in a position to compile a comprehensive job description which describes the responsibilities, objectives and principal tasks of the role. You will find a guide to writing job descriptions in Chapter 9.

A job description outlines what is required of the person performing the role. It is just as important to consider what sort of person is most likely to be effective in the role. A person specification is a document that sets out the skills, knowledge and experience required to perform the role effectively.

A person specification considers the:

- qualifications required
- essential skills and abilities
- desirable skills and abilities
- experience required.

In other words, what type of person are you looking for?

It is this step that is critical for organizations looking to improve their recruitment and selection procedures, and so boost their rates of staff retention. Many organizations spend a lot of time considering the requirements of the role and summarizing these in a job description. Far fewer consider the type of person that is likely to be effective in the role and summarizing this in a person specification. Yet this second stage can prevent many of the classic recruitment mistakes that organizations make, such as:

- appointing a graduate for an unskilled, low-level position – the graduates feels under-utilized and looks for alternative employment soon afterwards
- appointing someone with many years of relevant experience – they may need a new challenge, and tire quickly in the role
- promoting a good worker to a management position – this may well be the right thing to do, as promotion from within the organization is good, but there is no evidence to suggest that a good worker will automatically make a good manager
- appointing someone who is overqualified – you are looking for someone who is ideally qualified, with the appropriate experience; overqualified employees may become bored, or may even resent having to do a job that is 'beneath them'.

There are many more examples. By putting together a job description and a person specification, you are giving yourself the ideal platform for successful and effective recruitment and selection.

Internal recruitment

Now that you know the sort of person you are looking for, you need to consider where you will find them. Before you spend money on advertising the vacancy externally, have a look around you. Your new recruit may already be working within your organization. You might consider transferring or promoting an existing member of staff. You could advertise the vacancy internally on notice boards, in company newsletters, on the Intranet, or in company memos or circulars.

Perhaps you have temporary staff who may be interested in a permanent position? You may have part-time staff who are looking for a full-time role. Recruiting internally is not only effective. It is also highly motivating for all your employees if the organization is seen to promote and recruit from within.

External recruitment

If you have exhausted the possibilities of recruiting internally, it is time to look outside the organization. There are several alternatives.

Agencies and headhunters

Specialist recruitment agencies, or headhunters, offer a range of recruitment services that might suit your needs. You may know of an agency that specializes in your industry or sector, or you may have used a general recruitment agency in the past. If you are recruiting a senior member of staff, you may need the services of a headhunter. Headhunters tend to work in specialist sectors, recruiting for senior management and director level positions.

Using agencies and headhunters will rarely speed up the process of recruitment and selection. You need to brief the agency very carefully, and you will have to manage your relationship with the agency as closely as you would with a member of your own staff. But, as specialists, they may already have your ideal candidate on their books, and their professional service can save time with shortlisting, and even the first round of interviews if required.

Other external support

Your local job centre could help you in your search for the ideal recruit. Job centres offer a wide range of recruitment services, many of which are free of charge. You can find out more by visiting **www.jobcentreplus.gov.uk**.

If you are recruiting for several positions, you may find it useful to attend one of a growing number of local, regional or national job fairs around the country. Perhaps you or your organization are a member of a professional body, club or society that can help you to recruit your new member of staff? If you are looking for school or college leavers, then it may be worth contacting the careers officer at local secondary schools, sixth form and further education colleges.

Why not join the increasing number of organizations who recruit online? Specialist online recruitment sites enable applicants to read the job description and person specification, complete an application form and submit a CV, all online, and entirely electronically. There are thousands of online recruitment sites, but check out the websites of three of the largest:

- **www.monster.co.uk**
- **www.fish4jobs.co.uk**
- **www.workthing.com**

If you are not sure about using an online recruitment agency, there are other places online that might be suitable:

- your own website (particularly if it is well known, and gets a lot of visitors)
- national newspaper websites (if you place a recruitment advertisement in a national newspaper, it may well be repeated on the newspaper's own website).

Advertising

To be sure of attracting suitable candidates, you need to consider the wording of your advertisement very carefully. You need to state the essential requirements of the role clearly, but you must not sound inflexible so that you put off qualified candidates from applying.

Before you submit your advertisement, you need to check the wording thoroughly for any signs of discrimination. It is illegal to specify the preferred age, race or gender of the person you are looking for under any circumstances. If you are in any doubt, seek professional help. You may find the appendix on discrimination useful.

Think carefully about where you will place your advertisement. For some jobs, the local newspaper will be ideal. For specialist positions, perhaps a trade journal or newsletter would achieve the best results. For some roles, like marketing and sales positions, you may be better off advertising in the specialist recruitment section of a national newspaper. Wherever you decide to advertise, make sure that you specify precisely where in the newspaper you would like your advertisement to appear.

Shortlisting

Shortlisting effectively is vital to effective recruitment and selection. The technique that you use to shortlist candidates for interview can greatly influence your chances of recruiting the right person for the role. The response that you get to any recruitment advertisement will vary dramatically according to the following, and many other, factors:

- nature of role or position
- seniority of role or position
- perceived popularity of job
- organization's profile
- location of job
- salary and benefits offered
- time of year.

However large or small the response, you still need a fair and effective method for deciding which applications are worth considering, and which are not. You should start by considering how many candidates you can interview. For a small organization looking to appoint a new salesperson, shortlisting 6–8 candidates for interview is probably about right. For a large organization recruiting 25 new call centre staff, interviewing 100 might not be enough. How many is right for you?

If you plan to conduct the interviews alone, you should probably try to reduce the shortlist for interview to no more than about ten candidates. There are several methods for shortlisting effectively. A quick way to start is to reject the obviously unsuitable candidates. Usually you will receive a few applications that are clearly unsuitable, as with applicants who do not possess a skill or qualification that is essential for the role (for example, a driving licence). The next step is to compare each application with the job description and person specification that you created at the start of the recruitment process. You can legitimately reject those candidates who do not meet all the essential requirements specified in the advertisement.

One effective shortlisting method involves awarding points to each section of the application. You could score each one according to the following criteria:

Relevant work experience	max. 25 points
Desirable skills and qualifications	max. 25 points
Specific achievements	max. 10 points
Presentation of application	max. 10 points

You would then invite to interview those applicants who scored the highest points.

Interviewing

Having identified a shortlist of candidates, you need to consider the interview itself. There are several types of interview you could conduct, involving various people in your organization. Interview methods include:

Telephone interviews

You can use the telephone as a preliminary interview method to screen out unsuitable candidates, and to decide who you would like to interview face-to-face.

Face-to-face interviews

As the term suggests, these usually involve one interviewer and one interviewee. Traditionally they are the most common form of job interview. They are easy to organize, and are often fairly relaxed and informal. You can build rapport more quickly with a candidate if it is just the two of you.

Panel interviews

Panel interviews involve two or more interviewers with each interviewee. Normally, each of the interviewers has a specific role to play. For example, one member of the panel will question the candidate about their work experience. Another will talk about their interests outside work, and so on.

Serial interviews

Serial interviews comprise several one-to-one interviews in succession. Someone with a specialist interest conducts each of the interviews. A candidate may move from interview to interview in a single day, or over a number of days.

Multi-group interviews

This is when two or more interviewers meet with two or more shortlisted candidates. This method of interviewing is rarely used, but it can be very effective, particularly when gauging how candidates are likely to act as part of a team.

Interviewing candidates requires experience and specialist knowledge and skills. If you are new to recruiting, you should either seek professional assistance, or you should look for appropriate training.

Testing

For many vacancies, the process of shortlisting candidates from an application form or CV, then conducting one or more interviews, will be sufficient for making an informed appointment. However, it is increasingly common to employ a range of selection tests as part of the recruitment process. Selection tests fit broadly into one of the following categories:

- aptitude tests (testing appropriate skills or knowledge required for the position)
- intelligence tests (commonly known as IQ tests)
- personality tests (attempting to match a candidate's personality traits with those required of the job holder)
- work sample tests (asking the candidate to perform actual or realistic appropriate work tasks).

You will often hear cognitive or psychological tests referred to collectively as psychometric tests.

There are a number of personality tests available that are designed to predict how an individual candidate is likely to perform in a particular role or working environment. They range from the simple questionnaire to the complex psychological evaluation.

If you decide to include personality tests as part of your recruitment and selection process, you will require expert and professional help, both to administer the tests and to interpret the results. This is not a job for an amateur.

Selecting

If you have conducted interviews, and candidates have performed the selection tests required, you should be in a position to reduce your shortlist further for a follow-up interview, or even to select the most suitable candidate. Whether you conduct second interviews or not, once you have identified your chosen candidate you should move quickly to:

- make your job offer
- agree terms with your new employee
- issue a written offer of employment
- take up references
- reject unsuccessful candidates
- prepare to introduce your new employee into your organization.

Further advice

If you need help and advice with your recruitment process, there are plenty of books dedicated to the topic. This chapter serves merely as a sketch of the ideal recruitment model, and as an illustration of how recruitment and retention are closely linked. If you fail to recruit effectively, you are likely to recruit staff who will remain with you for less than a year. Rather than look for methods to retain the services of employees who were poorly recruited in the first place, look instead at your recruitment procedure. If you follow this simple recruitment model, you stand a much greater chance of recruiting and selecting employees that are suited both to your organization and the role that you need to fill.

Checklist

✓ Do you need to recruit at all? What are the alternatives?
✓ What position do you need to fill? Have you composed a job description?
✓ What type of person are you looking for? Have you composed a person specification?
✓ Can you recruit internally?
✓ Where externally should you recruit?

✓ Is your advertisement worded fairly and legally?
✓ What shortlisting methods have you put in place?
✓ What type of interview process should you use?
✓ What selection tests would work best?
✓ Do you need to conduct second interviews?
✓ Is this the right candidate?

06 new employees

In this chapter you will learn:

- **how to introduce new employees into your organization effectively**
- **what you need to prepare for your new recruit's first day**
- **how to establish an effective induction programme for all new employees**
- **the benefits that buddying and mentoring can bring to your organization**

We have already seen how the job of retaining staff begins right from the recruitment process. Having appointed the right person to fill your vacancy, you should do everything you can to introduce them into the organization effectively. First impressions count. This chapter looks at the steps you can take to make new employees welcome, and examines how an induction programme gives new employees the preparation they need by introducing them to the organization's culture and working practices. So what preparations can you make? How should you use your new recruit's first days with you? How can you introduce your new recruit effectively into your organization?

Welcome pack

Many organizations put together a welcome pack for new employees. A welcome pack provides all the information and paperwork that a new employee is likely to need. You might choose to send one to your appointed candidate at the same time as the letter offering employment. A welcome pack might contain some, or all, of the following items:

- terms and conditions of employment
- staff handbook or manual
- letter of introduction from Managing Director
- copy of health and safety policy
- details of where and when to arrive on the first day
- copies of organization's brochure or catalogues
- details of pension and health schemes
- what to bring in on the first day.

The aim of a well thought-out welcome pack is to excite the new recruit, to handle any administrative matters and to ensure that he or she is ready for the first day's employment.

The first day

Think about it. Can you remember your first day in a new job? Daunting, wasn't it? As the employer, you have a duty to make the first day run as smoothly as possible, and to make your new recruit feel welcome. First impressions last. If you do not make a new employee welcome, why would they want to stay with your organization? You cannot expect to retain good staff if you neglect them from the outset. So what can you do to prepare for the first day?

A good induction programme (see below) will include sensible provision for what the new recruit should do, and whom they should meet on their first day. Regardless of what is outlined in the induction programme, there are one or two steps that you can take that will demonstrate that the new recruit is both expected and welcome:

- Let the person at reception know that the new recruit is expected. Have any identity cards or badges ready for their arrival (if appropriate).
- Have a desk and chair ready, together with any stationery or other requirements. It's remarkable how many organizations leave this until after the new recruit has arrived.
- Try not to cover too much ground on day one.
- It sounds obvious, but make sure that you are actually in the office on your new recruit's first day.
- Have any administrative forms handy and ready for completion by the new recruit. Getting the administration out of the way makes a good use of the first day.
- Take time to catch up at the end of the day. How did your recruit feel the day went? Do they have any questions? Is there any feedback you can give them?

Staff handbook

Every organization will have its own idea about whether to issue a staff handbook and, if it does, what it should contain. A comprehensive staff handbook could include rules and regulations, company benefits (pensions, healthcare, etc.), the mission statement, extracts from the business plan, quotes from employees about what it is like to work for the organization, and so on.

If you have chosen to issue all employees with a comprehensive staff handbook, it ought to include a detailed section on training and development. The following might help when considering the training and development elements to be included:

Organizational framework
Objectives
Mission statement
Business plan

Individual employees

Principle of fitting in with objectives
Induction procedure
Job descriptions and their use
Appraisal policy
Who is responsible for training and development
Training and development opportunities
Equal opportunities policy

Induction

An induction programme is the process of introducing new employees into their jobs, and into the organization as quickly and effectively as possible. A well-structured induction programme makes new employees feel welcome, and encourages them to identify with the organization. Induction training of one sort or another takes place in every organization. After all, you show someone new where the kettle is, and make sure they know what time to arrive in the morning!

Increasingly, however, a detailed plan is set out covering what a new employee needs to know, what training and development he/she needs to do the job, who is responsible for teaching them, and over what timescale. Over a period covering the first few weeks in the organization, a new employee is introduced to the company, its staff and its structure. Administrative details, conditions of employment and rules and regulations will be covered. The new employee will meet the team or department he/she will work in, and will be introduced to each aspect of the new job. The best induction programmes are written and laid out as a checklist, showing clearly who is responsible for each element of training, with space for the new employee to sign or initial when each element has been covered satisfactorily. This way the new employee can see progression through the programme, and the manager responsible for training can monitor the progress made.

Try to strike a balance between formal and informal induction. The process becomes a bureaucratic farce if new employees have to sign a form to confirm that they know where tea bags are stored! The full induction programme checklist will vary from company to company, and from person to person. The following checklist is by no means exhaustive, but you might find it useful when planning your first induction programme.

Induction programme checklist

Introduction

Welcome to company
Explanation of induction programme
Organizational chart

Administration

P45
National Insurance number
Bank details
Brief introduction to accounts department
Complete staff record form
Complete season ticket loan form
Birth certificate/education certificates (if applicable)

Conditions of employment

Working hours (lunch hours, flexitime, overtime, bonuses, etc.)
Salary (when paid, how paid, how often reviewed)
Sickness/other absence (who to notify, doctor's certificate, statutory sick pay, etc.)
Holiday (number of days, who to notify, notice required, timing, bank holidays, carrying over holiday, etc.)
Notice period required
Disciplinary procedure
Union representation

Company

History (part of a group, when founded)
Finance (turnover, profitability, growth pattern)
Structure (number of employees, management structure)
Markets (customers, competitors, products, services)
Organizational objectives (mission statement, business plan)

Building and departments

Tour of building (canteen, coffee machine, toilets, photocopier, fax, e-mail, fire exits, notice boards, etc.)
Sales and Marketing department (structure, introduction to staff, function, objectives, etc.)
Customer Services department (structure, introduction to staff, function, objectives, etc.)
Other departments (structure, introduction to staff, function, objectives, etc.)

Rules and regulations
Smoking
Confidentiality
Security
Petty cash
Expenses

Health and Safety
Fire procedure
First aid
Protective clothing
Reporting accidents
Food and drink

Policy awareness
Equal opportunities policy
Race and gender discrimination policy
Maternity leave
Unpaid/compassionate leave
Alcohol and drugs
Discipline and grievance
Use of telephones (how to use them, how to answer them, personal phone calls)
Appearance and attitude
Addressing colleagues and superiors

Company benefits

Pension scheme (who qualifies, how to apply, brief outline, company contributions, etc.)
Health insurance (who qualifies, how to apply, brief outline, company contributions, etc.)
Company discounts
Clubs, societies and facilities
Share options
Company car/petrol allowance
Mortgage subsidy
Uniform/clothing allowance

The job
Introduction to department
Introduction to line manager

Function of department
Job description
How job fits into organizational objectives

Training

Training and development policy
Skills gaps identified
Appraisal policy and process

An extract from a sample induction programme is laid out overleaf.

Hints and tips for induction

- Plan an induction programme for each employee in advance. Use a general induction programme template if you have one, but tailor it to suit each new employee.
- Begin the induction programme with the letter that confirms the job offer: explain when to arrive, who to report to, what to wear, etc.
- Be realistic about what someone might reasonably take in each day. Fill the first day only with things that are absolutely necessary, for example, introduction to immediate colleagues only, smoking policy, etc.
- Build a new employee's confidence by giving him or her a small task on the very first day that will form part of their role.
- Offer a variety of ways of getting information across. Introduce some people as a team, others as individuals, go out to lunch with immediate colleagues, and so on. There is a lot of information to pick up, and a lot of faces to learn. Variety will make this easier.
- New recruits often learn more by shadowing other members of staff. They find it interesting, too.
- If you have a company handbook, don't assume that the new employee will have read and understood it. Go through it page by page if necessary.
- Make anyone new feel welcome by ensuring that they have a desk, stationery and a telephone ready when they arrive. This is absolutely essential!
- When putting the induction programme together, always consider who would be the most appropriate person to deliver each element of training.

Induction Programme for Marketing Co-ordinator

MONDAY 5 MAY

9 a.m.

Report to reception. To be met by David Carr, Marketing Manager, for initial introductions and a tour of the building.

10 a.m.

Meeting with the Marketing Team to meet Sarah Smith, Deputy Manager; Terry Jacob, Special Projects Manager; and George Koumi, Administrator. (Marketing Department Meeting Room)

11 a.m.

Meeting with Alex Pankhurst, Chief Executive. (AP's Office)

11.30 a.m.

Meeting with the Sales Team to meet David Todd, Sales Manager, Jane Howden, sales Co-ordinator, and Andrew Harris, Lisa Nnando and Nancy Hill, Customer Service Assistants. (Sales Meeting Room)

1 p.m.

Lunch with David Carr and Sarah Smith. (Meet in Reception)

2.30–5 p.m.

IT Training with Philip Kerr. An introduction to the company's Intranet and sales database. (IT Training Room)

TUESDAY 6 MAY

9 a.m.

Presentation by Terry Jacob on the Marketing Department's Special Projects. (Boardroom)

11 a.m.

Meeting with Jane Davies, Accountant, to confirm pay and tax details. (Accounts Department)

12 p.m.

Lunch with David Todd, Sales Manager. (Meet in Reception)

2–5 p.m.

Time in the Marketing Department.

WEDNESDAY 7 MAY

9 a.m.

Seminar by Simon Hunter, Production Department Manager. (Marketing Meeting Room)

11 a.m.

Meeting with John Rowe, Office Manager. (JR's Desk)

1 p.m.

Lunch with Barbara Jones, external Marketing Consultant heading the 'Road Promotion' Campaign. (Meet in Reception)

2 p.m.

Afternoon shadowing Sara Smith. (SS's Office)

THURSDAY 8 MAY

9 a.m.

Meeting with Catherine Chapman, Deputy Manatger HR Department, to explain the Health and Safety Rules and Company's commitment to IIP. (HR Department)

10 a.m.

Meeting with Anne Taylor, Training Manager, to explain training opportunities and to tour the Training Library. (Training Library)

12 p.m.

Lunch with Simon Hunter, Production Department Manager. (Meet in Reception)

2 p.m.

Time in the Marketing Department.

FRIDAY 9 MAY

9 a.m.

Time in the Marketing Department.

12 p.m.

Lunch with David Carr – induction debrief. (Meet in Reception)

2–5 p.m.

Visit to Harman Street Building. Tour by David Trump, Production Deputy Manager. (Harman Street Reception)

- Involve the Managing Director if you can (it makes a good and lasting impression) but not if there is a strong chance he or she will pull out at the last moment.
- Assigning a mentor to a new employee can be very worthwhile (this is someone who takes responsibility for the new recruit's welfare throughout the induction programme).
- Use the latter stages of the induction programme to go through the new employee's job description slowly and methodically. Ensure that he or she understands each section of it, and appreciates that it will form the basis of the appraisal at a later date.
- Give new employees a plan of the offices, with the names of the people in each room. Mark on the plan other useful features such as the toilets and kitchen. New employees feel very uncomfortable if they do not know their way around.
- Make sure that you send a memo around before a new employee starts. Tell everyone who is starting, when they start, what job they will do and, perhaps, what their background is. This will ensure that the new employee is welcomed on their very first day.
- Make sure that you, or the new recruit's line manager is in the office on the day they start work. If you are out of the office or, worse, on holiday, you are giving the new employee the impression that you are not really interested in them from the very first day.

Benefits of an induction programme

A well-planned induction programme for your newly appointed employee will provide many benefits:

- New staff will become effective employees over a much shorter period.
- There will be more staff motivation, and less staff turnover.
- New staff will understand their role within the organization, and what is expected of them.
- They will feel part of their department/team from the beginning.
- They will believe they are making a useful contribution towards the organization's objectives and goals.

There is no doubt that a carefully planned induction programme will have a positive effect on staff retention during the early stages of employment. Perhaps your organization has a poor staff turnover record during the first six months of employment. This is often caused by the new employee not feeling that they belong in the organization, or not appreciating or understanding the role that they play. Induction programmes are designed to help with both these issues. So if you do not already operate an induction programme for new employees, you should consider introducing one as a priority.

Case study

One company with which we are familiar tries to ensure that new employees do virtually nothing that will form part of their main role for the whole of their first week in the company.

New employees spend periods of one or two hours in each department, meeting each member of the team, and learning what they all do. One person acts as mentor throughout the first week, ensuring that the new employee is looked after, and also that he/she learns all the general company rules and regulations. A day out with one of the sales representatives is on the agenda, as well as a stint answering the phones (no matter how senior the new recruit is).

By the end of the first week, the new employee has a very firm grasp of how the organization works, and can begin in week two to learn about the specific role that he or she has been recruited for.

Buddying

Buddying is a method used to help new employees get accustomed to the culture, values and working practices of the organization. Buddying is a simple process of partnering a new employee with an existing member of staff for their first few days or weeks of employment. The buddy should be a reliable member of staff, who is a good role model for the organization. They should be someone who can remember, or empathize with, what it was like to be new, and who can understand the questions and difficulties that the new employee might face. A good buddy should play many roles:

- helping new employees to cope
- listening to their concerns and issues
- getting across the organization's values and culture
- offering advice
- providing a shoulder to lean on.

Some larger organizations have a formal buddying scheme in operation. A buddy is assigned to each new employee for the first month of employment, and longer term friendships and working relationships often result from this initial term. In other organizations, a buddying system of sorts is in place, but it is much less formal. An existing member of staff takes on the role of looking after the new employee, even though there is no formal requirement to do so.

The culture of your own organization may dictate whether or not you introduce a buddying scheme. If you do, you may know instinctively whether a formal or informal buddying scheme will work best for you. Whatever form it takes, buddying can make a new employee's introduction to the organization much less stressful, and can create long-term partnerships and friendships between the new employee and his or her buddy.

Buddying can influence staff retention in two important ways:

- It provides new employees with help and support during the first stressful days with the organization, when first impressions last.
- It can help build long-term partnerships and friendships that encourage employees to remain with the organization.

Mentoring

Mentoring is becoming extremely popular. In this context, a mentor is someone that an employee can refer to for advice and guidance when needed. Like buddies, they are there for new employees, but mentoring relationships tend to last over a longer period. Mentors tend to be more experienced, senior members of staff. As such, they tend to offer guidance on more strategic matters, rather than provide help with operational matters, which is more the role of a buddy. Mentoring relationships can exist well beyond a new employee's first few weeks of employment. In some organizations, every employee has a mentor to whom they may refer for guidance. Even the mentors themselves have someone to whom they, in turn, may refer.

Would introducing a formal or informal mentoring scheme work in your organization? Conducted effectively, mentoring relationships can be an important part of the infrastructure required to make an employee feel that they belong to the organization, and are valued.

Checklist

✓ Are you fully prepared for your new recruit's arrival?
✓ Have you prepared a desk or place for them to work?
✓ Have you devised a manageable first day?
✓ Do you have an induction programme in place?
✓ Have you thought about appointing a buddy for your new recruit?
✓ Would introducing a formal or informal mentoring scheme work in your organization?

07 investors in people

In this chapter you will learn:

- **what the Investors in People Standard is, and how it can benefit your organization**
- **how introducing certain training and development procedures will motivate and retain your key employees**

Investors in People is a national standard for developing your staff to meet your business objectives. This chapter explains what Investors in People is, what it involves, and how to be recognized as an Investor in People. It also considers the business and employee benefits of Investors in People, and how the Standard can motivate and retain your key staff.

What is Investors in People?

Investors in People is a National Standard for business development, the purpose of which is to set a level of good practice for improving an organization's performance through its people.

The overriding principle is straightforward:

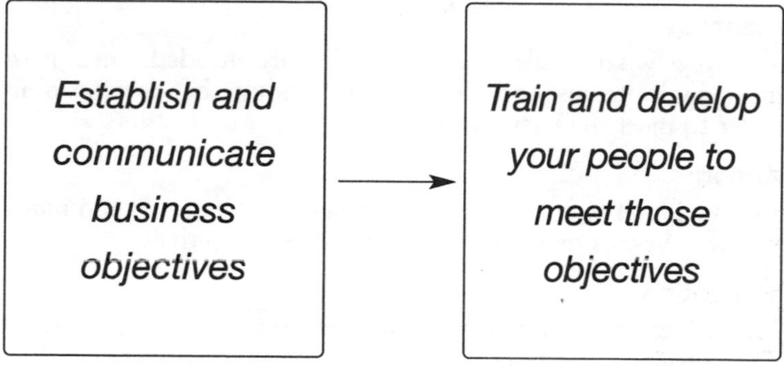

Investors in People emphasizes the importance of training and development. In particular:

- Training and development is linked and related to business planning, and to the overall business objectives of the organization.
- Training and development applies to everyone involved with the organization, including part-time staff and freelancers.
- Proper resources are allocated to training and development, and these resources are put to effective use.
- Improved business performance resulting from training and development is measurable.

The Investors in People Standard was established in 1990 by the National Training Task Force in partnership with leading business, personnel and employee organizations. It was piloted and tested during 1991 by Training and Enterprise Councils (TECs) and Local Enterprise Councils (LECs). The first review of the Standard was carried out in 1995, and the overall objectives of Investors in People were given strong praise and endorsement. The Standard has been improved and developed over the past decade, resulting in the revised Standard launched in 2000.

The four key principles

The Investors in People programme is based on four key Principles that should underpin the training and development practices of an organization:

Commitment

A commitment to invest in people to achieve business objectives.

Planning

Planning what skills and resources are needed, and how individuals, teams and departments should be developed in order to meet the business objectives.

Action

Taking action to train and develop people to provide and make use of the skills required to meet business objectives.

Evaluation

Measuring and evaluating the changes and improvements made as a result of training and development activity. Evaluating individual and team progress towards goals. Evaluating future needs.

The four key principles are broken down into twelve indicators, each of which an organization must demonstrate they follow in order to be formally recognized as an Investor in People. The principles and indicators are outlined on the following pages.

Commitment An Investor in People is fully committed to developing its people in order to achieve its aims and objectives.	
1 The organization is committed to supporting the development of its people.	Top managers are able to articulate the strategies in place to support the development of people in order to improve the organization's performance. Managers can describe specific actions that they have taken and are currently taking to support the development of people. People can confirm that the strategies and actions described do actually take place. All of the organization's people believe the organization is genuinely committed to supporting their development.
2 People are encouraged to improve their own and other people's performance.	People can give examples of how they have been encouraged to improve their own performance. People can give examples of how they have been encouraged to improve the performance of others.
3 People believe their contribution to the organization is recognized.	People can describe how the contribution that they make to the organization is recognized. People believe that their contribution to the organization is recognized. People receive appropriate and constructive feedback on a timely and regular basis.

Commitment (*continued*)	
4 The organization is committed to ensuring equality of opportunity in the development of its people.	Top management can describe strategies that they have put in place to ensure equality of opportunity in the development of people. Managers can describe specific actions that they have taken and are currently taking to ensure equality of opportunity in the development of people. People confirm that the specific strategies and actions described by top management and managers do actually take place and recognize the needs of different groups. People believe the organization is genuinely committed to ensuring equality of opportunity in the development of people.

Planning An Investor in People is clear about its aims and its objectives and what its people need to do to achieve them.	
5 The organization has a plan with clear aims and objectives which are understood by everyone.	The organization has a business/ operational plan with clear aims and objectives. People are able to explain and articulate the aims and objectives of the organization at a level appropriate to their role. Representative groups are consulted about the organization's aims and objectives.

Planning (*continued*)	
6 The development of people is in line with the organization's aims and objectives.	The organization has clear priorities which link the development of people to its aims and objectives at organization, team and individual level. People clearly understand what their development activities should achieve, both in terms of their own and the organization's objectives.
7 People understand how they contribute to achieving the organization's aims and objectives.	People can explain how they contribute to achieving the organization's overall business aims and objectives.

Action An Investor in People develops its people effectively in order to improve its performance.	
8 Managers are effective in supporting the development of people.	The organization ensures that managers have the knowledge and skills they need to develop their people. Managers at all levels understand what they need to do to support the development of their people. People understand what their manager(s) should be doing to support their development. Managers at all levels can give examples of actions that they have taken and are currently taking to support the development of people. People can describe how their managers are effective in supporting their development.

Action (*continued*)	
9 People learn and develop effectively.	People who are new to the organization, and those new to a job, can confirm that they have had an effective induction. The organization can demonstrate that people learn and develop effectively. People understand why they have undertaken development activities and what they are expected to do as a result. People can give examples of what they have learnt (knowledge, skills and attitude) from training and development activities. Development is linked to relevant external qualifications or standards (or both), where appropriate.

Evaluation An Investor in People understands the impact of its investment in people on its performance.	
10 The development of people improves the performance of the organization, teams and individuals.	The organization can show that the development of people has improved the performance of the organization, teams and individuals.
11 People understand the impact of the development of people on the performance of the organization, teams and individuals.	Top management understands the overall costs and benefits of the development of people, as well as its impact on performance. People can explain the impact of their development on their performance, the performance of their team, and of the organization as a whole.

Evaluation (*continued*)	
12 The organization gets better at developing its people.	People can give examples of relevant and specific improvements that have been made to development activities.

The Four Principles, and twelve Indicators of Investors in People are the Copyright of Investors in People UK and permission has been given for them to be used and reproduced in this publication. For further information, go to **www.investorsinpeople.co.uk**. You can order *The Standard*, and other Investors in People publications, from the IIP Orderline on 0870 850 4477.

How to be recognized as an Investor in People

The principles and indicators illustrated provide an excellent framework for developing your people, regardless of whether you seek formal recognition as an Investor in People or not. If you think your organization should formally apply to achieve the Standard, there are some specific steps that you should take:

1 Make sure that you understand the Investors in People Standard, as well as the human resources and strategic implications for your organization.
2 Undertake a review against the Standard to identify gaps in current practice.
3 Make the commitment to meet the Standard and communicate this commitment to all your staff.
4 Compile an action plan, and take action to bring about the changes and improvements required to meet the Standard.
5 Compile evidence of the measures and procedures in place that demonstrate that you meet the requirements of the Standard.
6 Arrange for a formal assessment from your local delivery organization – for most organizations this will be your nearest Business Link Centre.
7 Achieve recognition as an Investor in People.
8 Maintain the Investors in People Standard.

Business benefits

There are numerous business benefits associated with recognition as an Investor in People:

- It links training and development needs directly to the long-term aims of the organization.
- It provides a framework for future planning and strategy.
- It provides a structured method of improving the effectiveness of the organization's training and development.
- It gives individual employees a sense of ownership and responsibility for their training and development.
- It involves employees at all levels to get more closely involved in the business planning, and in the monitoring and evaluation of the results of training and development activities.
- It allows employees at all levels to be more aware of the overall business objectives, and the contribution they are making towards those objectives.
- It establishes a level of good personnel, and training and development practice.

Benefits to employees

Quite apart from the business and customer benefits, Investors in People recognition has a marked and measurable effect on the loyalty, motivation and retention of the organization's staff. These changes arise from a number of opportunities that Investors in People provides:

- increased job satisfaction
- a good working environment
- recognition and development
- greater involvement in working towards the organization's objectives
- better skilled and trained workforce
- higher staff morale
- improved adaptation to organizational change
- improved retention rates
- improved communication within the organization
- being part of a successful organization that recognizes its people.

From an employee's perspective, the framework that Investors in People provides is extremely motivating:

I understand what is required of my job.
↓
I know how my job contributes towards the objectives of my team.
↓
I know how my team's objectives contribute to the organization's overall business objectives.
↓
I know how to do my job.
↓
I have been provided with the training and development required to perform my job effectively.
↓
I can measure how well I am doing my job.
↓
I am given regular opportunity for measurement and feedback regarding the contribution that I make.
↓
I know what to do when things go wrong.
↓
I am led and guided by managers.
↓
I evaluate my personal and team performance at regular intervals.

Since the lack of training and development is often cited as the most popular reason why staff leave organizations, you may conclude that heading towards recognition as an Investor in People could be the single most important step you take to reduce staff turnover rates.

The evidence

There are currently over 34,000 organizations in the UK that have achieved formal recognition as an Investor in People, who together employ over 27 per cent of the UK workforce.

In a survey of just over 1,000 organizations employing five or more staff:

- 42 per cent of recognized organizations believe that the Investors in People Standard improved staff commitment.
- 26 per cent of recognized organizations believe that the Investors in People Standard improves employee relationships with management.
- 21 per cent of recognized organizations believe that the Investors in People Standard improved their productivity.
- 20 per cent of recognized organizations believe that the Investors in People Standard has helped improve staff retention.

(Source: Performance Tracking Research – *Business & Marketing Research*, October 2002)

Investors in People in practice

In order to achieve recognition as an Investor in People, there are few, if any, mandatory business or human resources procedures that you have to follow. Rather you must show evidence that your organization meets the needs and requirements of the twelve indicators that make up the four key principles. In practice, the way that you demonstrate this evidence will vary between organizations. For example, larger organizations are likely to need more formal objective setting procedures than, say, a small company with half a dozen employees.

Nevertheless, there are several training and development procedures that have been shown to improve performance, and to motivate and drive staff towards business objectives. Better still, an organization that introduces any of these procedures will have immediate and tangible evidence of their commitment to training and development, which will help in their quest for Investors in People recognition. So in the following chapters, we will consider: performance reviews/appraisals (Chapter 8); job descriptions (Chapter 9); training and development plans (Chapter 9); Personal Development plans (Chapter 9).

What it costs

It is very difficult to estimate what it costs for an organization to achieve Investors in People recognition. You need to consider cost in terms of:

- the time spent by you and your staff to introduce the changes required to meet the Investors in People Standard
- the costs of changing your business practices and procedures in order to meet the objectives of the Investors in People Standard (measured against the business benefits that those changes bring)
- the training and development costs that you will incur to equip your staff with the skills they need to achieve their individual objectives.

Of course, if you have all the evidence you need to demonstrate the way that your organization meets the requirements of the Investors in People Standard, you will not incur many of these costs. The only direct cost you will definitely incur is the cost of the assessment itself, when your organization is formally examined against the requirements of the Standard. Costs vary according to the size and complexity of the organization, but assessment is unlikely to take less than two days. Currently, you should assume a daily assessment charge of around £550 plus VAT.

Assuming that there are training and development procedures that you need to introduce into your organization, you may need professional assistance. Your nominated delivery organization can assist you, and can recommend a professional adviser if appropriate.

Once your organization is awarded Investors in People status, there is a programme of post-recognition reviews that you must pay for in order to retain the Standard. These are unlikely to be more frequent than every three years.

How to proceed

If you are interested in finding out more about Investors in People, or to start out towards official recognition, you should approach your local Learning and Skills Council or Business Link.

Training and development, or the lack of it, is regarded as a key motivation and retention factor by almost all employees. Being recognized as an Investor in People demonstrates a clear intention on your part to take training and development seriously, and at the same time provides the framework you need to empower your employees to deliver your business goals and objectives.

Checklist

✓ Are you committed to training and development?

✓ Is training and development linked to business objectives in your organization?

✓ Do your key employees understand how their role contributes towards their business objectives?

✓ Would being recognised as an Investor in People improve your ability to retain your key employees?

08 performance appraisals

In this chapter you will learn:

- **what a performance review or appraisal is**
- **about the types of appraisal system to consider**
- **how to conduct a performance appraisal**
- **about the business benefits of performance appraisals**

Performance appraisals get a bad press. Organized and managed effectively, performance appraisals are highly motivating, keeping staff target and goal driven, whilst encouraging training and development opportunities in the skills required for the role. Here, we outline what a performance appraisal system is and help you to decide what sort of appraisal system is suitable for your organization. You'll also learn about some of the common pitfalls associated with performance appraisal systems, and have a look at the link between appraising performance and retaining staff.

It must be said that there are many good books dedicated to helping organizations to define an appropriate performance appraisal system to suit their needs. Some suggestions for further reading are included on page 190. What follows, therefore, is not the last word on performance appraisals, but sensible and practical advice on getting the most out of a performance appraisal system, assuming you choose to adopt such a system at all.

Tip

In some organizations, the very word 'appraisal' is off-putting. Certainly the hit comedy series *The Office* has done nothing to enhance the appeal of conducting performance appraisals. If yours is such an organization, then think of a different name. Call it something more in keeping with your culture. How about 'performance review'?

What is a performance appraisal?

When you set business objectives (for example, to reach a turnover of £400,000 by the end of this year), it would be normal to take time to reflect at the end of the year on:

- whether you achieved your objectives
- the factors that meant you did not achieve it
- the level of shortfall
- what you could have done to reach your target
- what objectives you will set for next year
- how you plan to achieve those objectives.

It would not be unusual, therefore, to take the same approach with your staff. After all, you entrust them with responsibilities and key tasks that are linked to your organizational objectives. Without your staff, you would not be able to achieve your organizational objectives, however hard you worked yourself.

At the same time, your employees have their own opinions of how well they are working, whether they are contributing to the organizational objectives, and how you could help them to improve their contribution.

So a performance appraisal is a regular meeting with each of your staff, which provides many opportunities, including:

- to monitor the progress and achievement of the organization as a whole
- to plan for the continuing development of the organization
- to encourage and motivate employees to develop, and so increase, their value to the organization
- to identify training and development needs
- to identify potential performance
- to identify strengths and weaknesses in individuals, systems and procedures
- to assess the current level of job performance
- to assess the level and quality of support that an individual has received
- to gauge an individual's career aspirations.

All of these can be achieved if the time is taken regularly to conduct a two-way, positive, constructive and forward-looking discussion with each employee.

A good performance appraisal system will encourage employees to take on more responsibility for their own development in line with the organizational objectives. However, if an appraisal discussion achieves nothing else, it will seek to answer the following questions:

1 How are things going?
2 How could they go better?

Why appraisal systems get a bad press

Organizations often shy away from appraisal systems. They sound rigid, formal and bureaucratic. There are three very common reasons why appraisal systems fail:

Organizational culture

Training manuals which explain appraisal schemes often encourage you to adopt broadly similar, formal systems. However, the culture of every organization is different, and it is essential that you adopt a system that will fit in with the way you and your employees work.

If you have an informal working atmosphere then a formal appraisal system will not work well. It will seem out of place. Similarly, there is little point in trying to adopt a relaxed and informal appraisal system if the everyday working atmosphere is rigid and formal. It will be regarded as trivial and insincere. The skill is to adopt a system that suits your organization.

Bureaucracy

A lot of appraisal models require endless paperwork, for filling in and filing. This will only work if your organization is used to handling administration in this way. If not, then the appraisal process will soon be regarded as an administrative nightmare, and will be dropped at the earliest opportunity. There are several appraisal models which do not require such paperwork, so adopt one of these models if it is appropriate for your organization.

Different management styles

Consistency is important. It is essential that you train anyone who will conduct appraisals to do so. It sounds obvious, but many organizations do not take this elementary step. But think about it: why should your managers know how to appraise their staff? It is a skill that they might not have needed in their career so far.

Who should be appraised?

The simple answer is EVERYONE! Any system must be deemed fair and equal. If managers are not appraised like the other employees, then your staff will not buy into the appraisal process. They will resent appraisal, and see it as an opportunity for managers to check up on them. So:

- ensure that managers are appraised as well as other staff
- allow an opportunity for top management to be appraised in some way.

Self-assessment

Most books on the subject of performance appraisals discuss some sort of 'self-assessment form'. This is a sheet that the person being appraised completes before the appraisal discussion. Such forms can be very useful and productive, but you need to be very careful with how they are used. You will find an example of a self-assessment form below.

Performance review – self appraisal form

This form is designed to help you prepare for your discussion

Job holder:	Review period:
Job title:	Date of review meeting:
Main purpose of the job: *(refer to your job description)* Key performance areas: *(put in as many numbered areas as you identify in your job description)*	
My objectives for the last period:	Results:

Performance review – self appraisal form (*continued*)

What I did well and why
What I could have done better and why
What further training I require to perform my current role more effectively?
How I would like my role to develop in the future
How effectively do the relationships between me and my manager/other team members help me achieve my objectives?

Some books recommend that the person being appraised completes the self-assessment form prior to the performance appraisal, and hands it in before the appraisal meeting takes place. This can work, but some employees may feel that they are exposing their weaknesses and vulnerabilities by doing so. You may decide, instead, to request that each member of staff brings their completed self-assessment form to the appraisal meeting.

Here are some ways that a self-assessment form might be used:

1 As a means of preparation. The forms help employees to collect their thoughts and to plan what they want to say and what issues they want to raise.

2 As the appraiser, you could use the completed form as the basis for the performance appraisal discussion. This can have a very motivating effect on the employee because the appraisal discussion is therefore focused on the employee's agenda and issues.

Tip

Give the people being appraised every opportunity to voice their own concerns. It is remarkable how open and honest people are prepared to be about their own shortcomings.

Case study

A manager had to give an appraisal to a very difficult employee. Her main problem was that she was unable to make decisions or take responsibility for her actions. Her manager was dreading raising this with her as a problem that needed to be tackled. However, she arrived at the appraisal having identified this as a major barrier to her progress at work, and had entered this on her self-assessment form. What could have been a very difficult conversation became a very friendly and positive discussion.

How to conduct appraisals

The method you use for performance appraisal discussions will depend on the nature and culture of your organization. You may find the following pointers a useful starting point:

Plan

Give the employee at least a week's notice of the performance appraisal. This will allow enough time for him or her to:

- plan what he or she wants to say and achieve
- research any evidence/information required
- reschedule other work or commitments.

Purpose

Make sure that both the appraiser and the person being appraised know what the purpose of the discussion is. You might like to create a performance appraisal brief and give one to every employee in the organization. An example of a document you could distribute to all staff is illustrated below.

PERFORMANCE APPRAISALS

What is a performance appraisal?

A performance appraisal is an opportunity for you and your Department Manager to discuss your progress. It will look at how you are performing in your position. It will identify what you have done well and what your areas of weakness are. It will look at how you can improve your performance and what training or development would enable you to be more effective. It will also enable you to discuss how your own objectives relate to the Company's objectives.

What does it involve?

The appraisal will involve an in-depth discussion between you and your Department Manager. It may last a few hours and will give you the opportunity to express your views on the way you are working, as well as giving your Manager an opportunity to give you feedback.

What do I need to do to prepare?

The appraisal will give you an opportunity to express your views. You should therefore think about issues such as:

- What have you achieved since your last appraisal?
- What did you do well and why?
- What has caused difficulties?
- What training would help you be more effective?
- Are there areas of your role causing concern?
- How would you like your role to develop?

Your Department Manager will give you a form that you may wish to use to focus your thoughts.

What will the outcome be?
All appraisals will be different, but by the end you should have drawn up a list of objectives for the next six months and identified any training needs. A record of the appraisal will be kept in your staff file.

Will we talk about salary?
No. You will have a separate salary review. Your Department Manager will be able to give you more information about this.

Who should I talk to if I am worried about my performance appraisal?
Your Department Manager will be able to answer any questions about your appraisal. However, if you would prefer to speak to someone outside your department, then Harriet Dobson, Personnel Supervisor, will be able to advise you.

What should I do if I want to talk about my performance between appraisals?
Again your Department Manager will be able to answer any questions or Harriet Dobson, the Personnel Supervisor, will be able to advise you.

sample performance appraisal brief

Organizational objectives

Always relate the appraisal discussion back to the organizational objectives.

Have in your mind:

- the mission statement
- the business plan
- the department goals.

Questions

Ask open-ended questions where possible. The discussion is designed to be positive. Asking lots of closed questions creates an atmosphere which is negative and unfriendly. Try to encourage the person being appraised to give opinions. For example, ask: *'Why do you think you missed the deadline for the Daily Mail promotion?'* rather than, *'Did you miss the Daily Mail promotion deadline because you did not plan your time carefully?'*

Appraise the appraisal

The final stage of any appraisal discussion should be to review how it went. Did it go as you both expected? Did you cover all the ground you expected to? How would you do it differently next time?

Targets

Refer back to the objectives and targets set at the last appraisal discussion. Set targets and objectives for the next period. You may wish to use an appraisal summary form to record the targets and objectives that you have set. You will find an example of a performance review summary form opposite.

Remember that all objectives you set should be SMART:

Specific
Measurable
Achievable
Realistic
Timebound

Follow-up appraisals

At the second and subsequent appraisal, the appraiser should be looking for answers to the following questions:

1 How was the employee performing at the last appraisal?
2 How has the employee improved upon that performance?
3 How will the improvement continue?

Tips

- Concentrate on the employee's *role*, rather than their *personality*. You are not trying to unearth character defects, so you need to concentrate on actions rather than behaviour.
- As an appraiser, you are looking for three things in an employee:
  1 *Job-related performance:* how an employee does his/her job.
  2 *Company-related performance:* how an employee's job relates to the organizational objectives.
  3 *Person-related performance:* an employee's potential.

Performance review – summary form

Job holder:	Review period:
Job title:	Date of review meeting:
What changes in the purpose and/or key performance areas did you agree?	
What agreements were reached in respect of the performance of objectives and/or conduct or behaviour?	
What did you agree as training needs? *(any training needs should be expressed in the form of outcomes, i.e. 'By the end of the training I should be better able to …')*	
What had the job holder identified as having done well, and not?	

Performance review – summary form (*continued*)

What did you agree regarding future developments?
What did you agree about objectives for the next period?
What did you agree about interface with others in the team?

Appraising Manager____________________ Date ________

Appraisee's comments ____________________

This appraisal has been discussed with me:

Signature ____________________ Date ________

Manager's signature ____________________ Date ________

Where to appraise

Although this will depend largely on the type of appraisal system you have chosen to adopt (formal/informal), there are nevertheless several pointers that might help you:

Neutral territory

Try to ensure that the place where the appraisal discussion takes place is neutral, and does not give either party the upper hand. The Manager's office, for example, might well intimidate the person being appraised and create the wrong atmosphere from the start.

Quiet

There is nothing more off-putting than trying to hold a serious discussion while the phone rings constantly or people keep interrupting. You must ensure that the discussion takes place where you will not be disturbed.

Tip

If you break off from the discussion to answer the telephone, you give the employee the impression that their appraisal is unimportant.

Public places

If you have chosen to adopt an informal performance appraisal system, then a café or restaurant might seem like the perfect venue for the appraisal discussion. Resist this temptation. Noise and the process of eating stifle progress and get in the way.

Seating arrangements

Wherever you decide to hold the discussion, make sure that you do not sit directly opposite each other. Psychologically, this creates an impression of confrontation from the start.

When to appraise

It is important to find a time when:

- it is convenient for both the appraiser and the person being appraised
- it is likely to be quiet and less pressured.

Try not to pick a time when the company is busy, such as:

- month end
- sales period end
- holiday period.

Allow plenty of time

Performance appraisal discussions take a long time. You may well need an average of half a day with each employee. Looking at your watch every ten minutes is very off-putting, and gives the person being appraised the impression that the discussion is not important. So make sure that your diary is clear in case an appraisal takes longer than you anticipated.

Conduct appraisals regularly

Annual appraisals are rarely appropriate. Trying to appraise a year's work and contribution in the space of a morning is not likely to succeed. So appraise more frequently. Twice a year is about right for formal appraisals, and more regularly if your appraisal system is informal. The key is to appraise as often as you feel you need to for your organization.

Tips

- If you are running out of time, then do not try to cram everything you needed to cover into the remaining time. Cover as much as you can thoroughly, and then put another date in the diary straight away to complete the appraisal.
- Strike a balance in the discussion between the positive and the negative, and between the past and the present. Remember that to dwell on the work done for too long will seem very negative: you should be drawing on the past to plan ahead for the future.
- Plan and book an appraisal discussion well in advance. This helps to reinforce the importance of the appraisal, and gives both parties plenty of time to prepare. Once booked, there should be nothing so important that you need to cancel the discussion – it gives the person being appraised a very bad impression.
- Performance appraisals take a long time. Allow for a ten-minute refreshment break about halfway through.
- Provide plenty of pens, paper and other stationery for both appraiser and person being appraised to take notes.

- Make sure you read the employee's job description thoroughly as part of your preparation.
- You need to understand the employee's role in order to conduct the performance appraisal properly.
- Do not look at individual tasks – look at achievements.
- Be realistic about what has been achieved and what is achievable.

Salary reviews

There are different opinions about this. However, a majority say that you should leave a salary review for another occasion. If you discuss salary, you may find the following happening:

1 Employees only listen to the objectives, achievements or targets that you set in terms of the impact they have on their salary.
2 Employees will be reluctant to be honest about anything that they could have improved for fear that it will affect the size of their salary rise.

It is better to divorce the salary debate from the appraisal discussion. This is another reason for holding appraisals more than once a year. It is more difficult to stave off the salary debate if you only review performance annually.

Benefits of appraisals

- They provide evidence of how you and your employees are contributing to the business, and what else you still need to do.
- They provide the basis for tying in individual performance with business objectives.
- They produce more motivated employees.
- They provide an important communication channel for retaining key staff.
- They identify training and development needs.
- They give employees the chance to voice views and opinions on the development of themselves and of the organization.
- They enhance the relationship between a manager and his or her staff.
- They relate the effectiveness of an employee's contribution to the effectiveness of the organization as a whole.

Checklist

- ✓ Are appraisals appropriate for your organization?
- ✓ What sort of appraisal system will you adopt?
- ✓ How will you use appraisals to improve motivation and staff retention?

09 training and development

In this chapter you will learn:

- **how to compile a job description**
- **about the importance of personal development plans**
- **how to make more effective use of training and development**
- **about introducing training plans**
- **how to establish training and development objectives**

In Chapter 7, we considered how Investors in People provides an ideal framework for improving your organization's performance through your people. To achieve recognition as an Investor in People, you must show evidence that your organization meets the needs and requirements of the four key principles of commitment, planning, action and evaluation. The way that you demonstrate this evidence will vary between organizations. Nevertheless, there are several training and development procedures that have been shown to improve performance and to motivate and drive staff towards your business objectives. Better still, an organization that introduces any of these procedures will have immediate and tangible evidence of their commitment to training and development, which will help in their quest for Investors in People recognition. In Chapter 8, we considered the use of performance reviews, or appraisals. In this chapter, we consider the retention benefits of job descriptions; personal development plans; training plans.

Job descriptions

A job description is an essential tool in the recruitment and retention process. At its most simple level, a job description outlines the main purpose, tasks and responsibilities of the position. Managers are often guilty of compiling a job description in a hurry or, worse, skipping this stage altogether. But compiling a job description will pay dividends because:

- when recruiting, it helps you to focus on the skills, knowledge and experience required to do the job
- it helps you to draft the wording used in a recruitment advertisement
- it will give you a tool against which to shortlist candidates
- throughout a term of employment, a job description helps both you and the employee to focus on what is required of the jobholder, where the priorities lie, and what training and development is required to do the job
- it is an important document to refer to and update during a performance review/appraisal.

Used properly, you will update a job description over time, in line with the changes and development of the role.

If your organization takes training and development seriously, and has a training and development plan, you may find that there is a specific formula that all employees must follow when compiling a job description. If so, you must follow the formula, as a job description will be referred to during appraisal, grievance and discipline procedures, so it is vital that it is sufficiently robust, and matches your organization's needs. If there is no company formula to follow, you may find the following short guide to job descriptions useful.

Simple job descriptions

A simple job description should summarize the basic requirements and conditions of the role. In most cases, you will probably be able to restrict this summary to a single sheet of paper. A simple job description should include:

Job title

Make sure that this is simple and unambiguous. Often companies use titles that make jobs sound more important than they are. There is little to be gained from this, and it can lead to confusion. So, if it is a junior role, compile a job description for a Sales Assistant, rather than a Sales Executive. Or Telephonist, rather than Customer Services Operative.

Job location

If the role requires travel, or working on several sites, then this should be stated. You may wish to keep all options open by stating that the role may require a move to another site at a later stage.

Who the jobholder reports to

Use the line manager's title, rather than name. This will ensure that job descriptions always remain focused on roles, rather than the personality of the people performing those roles.

Job purpose, tasks and responsibilities

These should be listed simply and clearly. A basic job description will outline the key tasks and responsibilities only, to maintain the brevity of the document. When recruiting, this will also ensure that prospective candidates focus on their suitability to perform the most significant tasks of the role. Never use in-house or industry jargon to describe a task, and always spell out acronyms in full. For example, say *Sales Order Processing*, rather than *SOP*. The idea is to make a simple job description as clear and helpful as possible.

Hours required, grade and holiday entitlement

If the role demands normal office hours, then these should be stated. To some, office hours mean 9.30 a.m. to 5 p.m; to you, it might mean 8.30 a.m. to 6 p.m. Build in some flexibility for working outside normal working hours on occasions. Perhaps you will need this person to work late when preparing for an annual sales conference, for example.

A job description that you have compiled should be signed and dated by you. This will indicate when the job description here was last updated, and who compiled it. We have included a sample, basic job description that might assist you when compiling your own.

PORTER COMMUNICATIONS LTD

JOB DESCRIPTION

Job Title: Office Manager
Reporting to: Managing Director

Purpose of Job:
To manage the office, and the everyday administrative functions of the company. To manage the secretarial services provided, and to ensure an efficient customer service to clients and members of the public.

Principal Responsibilities:

1 Manage a team of eight secretarial and administrative staff with responsibility for word processing, filing, customer service, postal services, switchboard and reception.
2 Compile weekly staff schedules, and monthly statistical reports for senior management.
3 Manage systems for purchasing of office stationery and supplies, negotiating with local suppliers to ensure optimum value for money.
4 Supervise agency cleaning staff to ensure cleanliness and hygiene within all office areas.
5 Other administrative and secretarial services as required by the Managing Director from time to time.

Experience and Knowledge Requirements:

1 Substantial administrative experience and a proven track record in people management.
2 Excellent computing and word processing skills, as well as experience of telephone and switchboard systems.
3 Outstanding verbal and communication skills.
4 Education equivalent to two 'A' Levels.

Sample simple job description

Tips

- The most difficult sections to write are often the overall purpose of the job and the principal duties. Try to summarize the principal duties first before attempting to describe the overall purpose. If you identify the principal duties, you will find that they provide an ideal basis for encapsulating the main purpose of the job
- Try to use appropriate, well chosen 'action' verbs to describe the key tasks and responsibilities. You may find the following list useful:

clerical:	check make available operate provide maintain submit present
senior specialist:	analyse proposed interpret advise appraise recommend develop
line management:	plan direct establish implement achieve ensure maintain set review

Longer job descriptions

Many organizations use job descriptions for ongoing appraisal of the jobholder, as well as for the initial recruitment and selection process. If this is the case in your organization, then the simple, one-page job descriptions are unlikely to be sufficient.

For appraisal purposes, you really need a job description that lists not only the key responsibilities, but also the individual objectives and tasks that make up each responsibility. For example, let's look at the role of an editor in a publishing company. The principal task might be to monitor the stock and financial performance of a series of books. In a simple job description, the responsibility would be listed simply:

Key responsibility

Monitor the stock and financial performance of the DIY Gardening Series.

But when it comes to the appraisal, how will you judge whether this task has been completed satisfactorily or not? Is it enough to monitor stock levels once a year? Once a month? Once each day? Is there a minimum stock level that must be maintained at all times? Is there a maximum stock value that must not be exceeded?

A longer job description provides clarification for each responsibility, ensuring that the role can be appraised at any time in a fair and unambiguous way. So, the example above might look like this:

Key responsibility

Monitor the stock and financial performance of the DIY Gardening Series:

- monitor stock levels on a weekly basis
- agree reprint quantities with Publishing Director
- ensure appropriate text corrections are made
- arrange reprint with Production Manager
- inform customer services department and marketing team of schedules

Check the following at least monthly:

- sales performance of list
- ongoing editorial and production costs

Report monthly to Publishing Director on sales and costs.

You need to think carefully about whether to spend time developing a longer job description for each role. There is no doubt that such a job description would assist both the recruitment and ongoing assessment of the jobholder, but they can be very challenging to write. It is not always possible to define, in simple terms, the tasks that make up every

MARKETING ASSISTANT

INTRODUCTION

The main thrust of the Marketing Assistant's role is to provide support and information to the sales and marketing function. The Marketing Assistant reports to the Sales & Marketing Director, but also supports the Customer Services Manager and the Home Sales Manager. The Marketing Assistant is expected to manage his/her own agenda, within a framework set by the Sales & Marketing Director.

AREAS OF RESPONSIBILITY

1 Communication

Routine information provision between the marketing department and other departments within the company, between the company and its trade sales force, between the company and its UK trade customers, and between the company and its overseas customers, agents and distributors world-wide.

Detailed Breakdown

1.1 Compile and distribute amongst all staff short weekly memos outlining the campaigns that the marketing department is currently engaged in, using information provided by Departmental Managers.

1.2 Provide weekly memos for the trade sales force and *ad hoc* reports as requested by the Home Sales Manager using information provided by the Customer Services Manager.

1.3 Update trade customers with details of new products and services using information provided by Departmental Managers and the Customer Services Manager.

1.4 Provide monthly product release schedules to Trade Representatives.

1.5 Provide printouts for Trade Representatives as requested, and information from the customer database as requested by the Home Sales Manager.

1.6 Compile and distribute a monthly memo of other relevant information for Trade Representatives using information provided by the Customer Services Manager and the Home Sales Manager.

1.7 Ensure that sample products are sent to the trade sales force, trade customers and overseas agents and distributors.

1.8 Compile and distribute a composite memo by 10th of each month to all agents and distributors world-wide using information provided by Departmental Managers and the Customer Services Manager.

1.9 Proof-read all promotional literature generated by Marketing Department.

Full job descriptions can be used as a basis for performance appraisal responsibility. Even if you can, a job description is likely to be several pages long.

Ultimately, the type of job description you use may be directed by the environment and culture of the organization that you work for. However, whether you use the shorter or longer format, a clear, unambiguous job description is an essential tool in the recruitment and selection process, and you should allow time to compile one as thoroughly as you can.

Personal development plans

Personal development plans are documents that commit to paper each individual employee's contribution to the business. They outline the link between an employee's personal development and the development of your organization. They set desired performance standards and the training on offer to achieve those standards, together with a target date. Personal development plans are not a requirement of Investors in People, but they are useful, focused documents that can be used in several ways:

1 As a document which expands and broadens the scope of a basic job description. If you have chosen to use very simple, one-page job descriptions, you might consider introducing Personal development plans.

2 They encourage employees to identify the link between the roles they play, the overall business objectives and the training and development actions needed to achieve them.

Personal development plans are normally short, unambiguous written documents. You will find a simple template for a personal development plan opposite.

If you are using longer job descriptions already, personal development plans summarize the training and development available to ensure that an employee is able to fulfil each aspect of his or her role. Compiling and reviewing the contents of a personal development plan should be an important part of the performance appraisal process (see Chapter 8).

If a job description outlines what an employee's role is, a personal development plan sets objectives and goals for the employee's training and development needs to fulfil this role.

A good personal development plan includes specific objectives or standards to be reached, together with a desired achievement

Personal development plan

Name: Division: Department:		Manager: Date:	
Area of activity	Standard to be achieved	How?	By when?
			Review date:

date. Both of these features are extremely important because they make a personal development plan a living and constantly evolving document.

If you use personal development plans, you must make sure that you and your employees refer to them regularly. Their benefit lies in their ability to take a snapshot of an employee's training and development needs, and to create the link between business goals and this training and development. Make sure that they are used as part of the performance appraisal process, or they will lose their value and credibility very rapidly.

Making better use of training

Using personal development plans gets more out of your employees than simply sending them on a series of training courses. Primarily, they are personal documents, which focus on the training and development needs of an individual employee. They are compiled and updated through the joint commitment of both the employee and his or her line manager. They are designed to reflect the needs and aspirations of the employee over the short, medium and longer terms. A personal development plan should concern itself as much about an employee's long-term development, as about their short-term training needs.

So how do you identify what should be included in a personal development plan? In most organizations that use them, it is the responsibility of an employee's line manager to work with them to compile the personal development plan. It should be noted that the employee's line manager may require the appropriate training to ensure that they can work with the employee to compile the personal development plan effectively. This training requirement should be built into the line manager's own personal development plan. There are courses available to develop the skills that are required, such as counselling, mentoring and coaching. Alternatively, you may have senior managers in your organization who could deliver such training internally.

A straightforward way to identify the particular development needs of an individual employee is for the line manager and employee to complete a simple questionnaire. An example of such a questionnaire is laid out opposite:

Personal development plan questionnaire:

What elements of your work do you most enjoy?

What elements of your work do you least enjoy?

Which elements would you most like to improve?

Do you think you are given enough responsibility in your role?

In what areas would you like more responsibility?

What is preventing you from developing as you would like to within the organization?

What interests or skills would you like to develop?

Which skills are most likely to improve your work performance?

How do you prefer to learn?

What skills, abilities or experience would help you to feel more confident at work?

What are your hobbies or interests that you would most like to develop outside work?

The answers to these questions will help you to set objectives for the personal development plan. Having completed the questionnaire, the next skill required is to match the employee's own objectives with the business objectives of your organization. There is no obligation for the organization to commit to developing a skill or aptitude that does not contribute towards the business objectives, although you should consider the effect that such a commitment would have on the individual employee. Some organizations take the view that developing an employee in areas that are not core to their business objectives, nevertheless has a positive, motivating effect on the employee.

For example, you may have an employee who has a particular hobby or interest. The employee may not be able to commit time to this interest because of work commitments. As part of a personal development plan, you may be able to offer support in certain ways:

- the time to pursue this hobby or interest (for example, a sport or team game)
- financial support to cover the cost of training courses to develop skills that are not core to the organization (for example, a degree or other qualification).

The principle is that providing support of this kind to the employee is likely to have two key benefits:

1 they will be more motivated (because you are providing them with the opportunity to develop non-core interests)
2 they are likely to remain with the organization (after all, what other employer would support their hobby or interest?)

As well as supporting hobbies and interests, there are other personal development opportunities you might wish to support that are not core to business objectives:

- learning to drive
- giving up smoking
- losing weight
- improving language skills.

The benefit to your organization is having an employee who is healthier, happier or more accomplished.

Setting objectives

Whether you propose to support non-core development or not, the skill is to identify a number of key development objectives for each employee. They must be agreed by both the employee concerned, and his or her line manager, otherwise the plan will not be useful. Personal development plans are positive, motivational documents, so if there is an objective that an employee disagrees with, it will reduce the effectiveness of the personal development plan.

As with all training and development, reviewing and evaluating progress with the objectives set out in a personal development plan is essential. You could discuss progress with each employee as part of their performance review/appraisal (see Chapter 8).

Training plans

Your business plan, if you have one, outlines strategic goals and objectives for a given period (often one year). In order for training and development to be relevant, targeted and appropriate for your employees, you will need to frame your business objectives in terms of the training and development that will be required to meet them.

For each business objective, you should consider:

- where you are now
- where you want to be
- what skills and experience you have available
- what additional skills will be required
- which staff require training and development
- by when?

By answering these questions, you can compile a training and development plan that directly links business objectives with the people who will meet them (which will provide important evidence if you are heading towards recognition as an Investor in People). Since inappropriate or insufficient training and development is one of the major causes of staff turnover, this training plan will ensure that your employees:

- are adequately trained to perform their role
- understand how their role contributes to the overall business objectives.

The training plan amply illustrates your commitment to training and development. Provided that progress is reviewed and evaluated at regular intervals, you should ensure that few employees cite the lack of training and development as a contributory factor towards their leaving.

You will find a sample extract from a training plan below.

Extract from training plan:

Business objective:
To increase repeat sales of consumer product range by 15% by end of December 2004.

Current situation:
Business to new customers has risen by 5% during 2003. But repeat business has fallen by 7.5%. Sales team have concentrated on attracting new business, at the expense of building relationships with customers and meeting their ongoing needs.

Skills available:
JE has a proven track record in gaining repeat business from customers in his territory. PB has good networking skills. Both could be involved with internal training.

Skills required:

1 Post sale relationship management

Required by:	28 February 2004
For whom:	JS, PB, EP, DS and TE
Delivered by:	APT Training

2 Cross selling and up-selling skills

Required by:	31 March 2004
For whom:	JS, PB, EP, DS and TE
Delivered by:	JE (internally)

3 Networking within customer organizations

Required by:	28 February 2004
For whom:	JE, JS, EP, DS and TE
Delivered by:	PB (internally)

Checklist

- ✓ Do you use job descriptions in you organization?
- ✓ Will you use short or longer job descriptions?
- ✓ Do you take the opportunity to review the job description during appraisals?
- ✓ How do you link training and development with business objectives?
- ✓ Do you do enough to encourage non-core activities?
- ✓ Could you support your employees with training and development in non-core interests and activities?
- ✓ If you have a business plan, do you also have a training plan that outlines the training and development required to meet the business objectives?

part three

money, motivation and benefits

10 salary packages

In this chapter you will learn:

- about strategies for setting an appropriate salary
- how to avoid making pay a demotivating issue
- about the types and benefits of bonus and commission schemes
- about the merits of retention benefits

A competitive, balanced remuneration package will help you to attract suitable employees with the skills required to contribute towards the fulfilment of your business objectives. An unattractive remuneration package will make recruitment of the right staff very difficult, and holding on to them harder still. This chapter explains how to approach the issue of remuneration, and how to design a remuneration package that will attract and retain the best employees for your needs.

The market rate

A very successful businessman once gave me this simple piece of advice: If you want to recruit motivated, loyal employees, then you should pay the 'staying rate' not the 'going rate'. In other words, the 'going rate' is what everyone else pays. That's fine, if the skills required are easy to find. But recruitment and retention are expensive. An employee can leave an organization for many reasons. By paying a little more than the 'going rate' you will ensure that an employee leaves for a reason beyond your control, rather than just to work for your competitor for a higher salary.

It goes without saying that in order to pay the 'staying rate', you need to know what the 'going rate' is. What is the market rate for the level of employee in question? What would your main competitor offer an employee at a similar level? If you are not sure, see if you can find recruitment advertisements in newspapers and professional journals for similar roles in comparable organizations. Does a professional body or society publish industry specific surveys on salaries and pay scales? If you are still in doubt, consider the levels of skill required to perform the role.

- If the role demands few skills, then you could ask for advice from a general employment agency, or the local job centre.
- If specific skills are required to perform the role, then the national press may hold the key. Most national newspapers have industry or role-specific recruitment sections on each day of the week. For example, the *Guardian* has a sales and marketing recruitment section every Monday. You could compare the salaries offered for similar roles in other organizations.
- If highly specialized skills are needed, then you should start with professional journals, and industry bodies and societies.

Some have specific recruitment sections, which may indicate the market rate for the role in question. Others publish annual salary data which may give you an idea about whether you pay above or below average for your industry or sector.

Having established the market rate, you may not feel comfortable with following the successful businessman's advice, and paying the 'staying rate' without further consideration. However, some thought about the role, and the person who is performing it, should help you to establish the rate you should pay:

- Pay above the market rate if you have a higher than average calibre of employee performing the role.
- Pay above the market rate if you have an employee that you are keen not to lose to a competitor organization.
- Pay above the market rate if the skills required for the role are in short supply.
- Pay at or below the market rate if the skills required for the role are plentiful.

Basic pay

Basic pay is set by law, and the national minimum wage in the UK is currently £4.50 per hour. You can pay whatever salary you like above this rate, but you cannot legally pay less. What you pay can be broken down into a number of constituent parts:

Type of pay

Would your employee work more effectively, and be more motivated, if they were paid by the hour, or paid an annual salary? What is more likely to retain the employee – paying a salary according to the time committed to the organization, or a salary based on performance? Would this employee be motivated by pay based entirely on commission? Different employees will be motivated in different ways, so you may need to consider how best to pay each of your key employees. For example, a salesperson is likely to be target driven, and switched on by commission based pay.

If your aim is to retain a shareholder, then it is usually more tax efficient to pay out cash as share dividends. Currently, dividends incur tax above £35,000, but do not incur National Insurance.

Speak to your accountant about the best ways to pay directors and shareholders.

Pay structure

Whatever pay structure you adopt, it should be fair, and it should make sense. Under new legislation, for example, a part-time employee should be paid at the same rate as a full-time colleague, on a pro rata basis. Employees should consider that their salary is fair, both in relation to their colleagues, and to comparable roles in other organizations. Many organizations adopt published salary scales. When recruiting, the organization has the flexibility to recruit someone who needs further training and development, and pay at the bottom of the salary scale, or the organization can recruit an experienced worker at the top end of the salary scale.

Overtime

Some organizations have a real problem with overtime. They specify fixed working hours to some staff, paying overtime for hours worked in excess of the stated hours, but they do not set fixed hours for other staff, and expect them to commit extra hours as and when required. This often leads to demotivated employees who witness their colleagues earning valuable overtime, while they are expected to work the extra hours for nothing. Give some thought to the role that overtime is going to play in your organization, for example, who will qualify for it, and how you will pay for it.

The demotivating effect of pay

There are several common mistakes that organizations make regarding pay. Any of these scenarios regarding salary and pay may actually demotivate your employees:

- paying higher rates of salary in order to attract a higher calibre of new employees – this can be demotivating for existing employees, who have worked hard and shown loyalty in order to reach their salary levels
- offering salary increases when an employee threatens to resign – you are, in effect, rewarding your employee's disloyalty
- paying significantly less than the competition.

Bonuses and commission

Bonus and commission payments can be highly motivating and can have a significant incentive effect. However, you must ensure that bonuses and commissions are treated as extra payments to employees, otherwise they will quickly be treated as part of their basic pay, and will be taken for granted. If that happens, the bonus payment loses its incentive effect very quickly.

Incentive payments of any kind should be linked to business goals and objectives, and should be paid, where possible, on the achievement of specific individual targets. The principle is that an incentive pay scheme should motivate employees to work more effectively to achieve their own individual targets, which in themselves contribute towards the overall business objectives. Incentive pay is an effective method for motivating, recognizing and encouraging the results that your employees achieve.

To establish an effective scheme, begin by deciding upon the business results that you want your employees to deliver. Then you can turn them into SMART (**S**pecific, **M**easurable, **A**chievable, **R**ealistic, **T**imebound) company, team and individual objectives. Targets and objectives should be challenging but achievable. Some examples of SMART targets or objectives are as follows:

- selling 250 widgets in the three month period October–December, of which 100 should be to new customers
- in the call centre, reducing the number of missed calls to less than 1 per cent within four weeks.

There should be no ambiguity about whether an objective has been achieved or not. It is demotivating to have to argue with an employee about whether or not a bonus or commission payment has been earned. You also need to consider who you will offer incentive pay schemes to. It makes sense to offer such schemes to employees who are able to influence the objectives that you want to achieve directly. However, there is a danger of alienating other employees if you only decide to reward a certain team or department.

In some organizations, there is a feeling of suspicion amongst employees that the business targets on which bonuses will be paid are designed to be all but unachievable in order to keep bonus payments to a minimum. If you spot this feeling amongst your own staff, the easiest way to handle it is to involve them in the process of establishing budgets, targets and goals. If your employees feel that they have been involved in the budget-setting process, they will regard the reaching and beating of targets as even more motivating.

Another golden rule is not to be tempted to cap a bonus or commission payment. It can have an instant and long-lasting demotivating effect, as the case study below illustrates:

Case study

At a well-known publishing company, sales reps were paid a commission on all book sales in their territory. The commission rates were set at a rate such that, in an average year, reps might reasonably earn an extra £4000–£6000 if they reached the territory targets they had been set. One year, the company decided to try selling books direct to the trade by mail order. This proved successful, and resulted in a 40 per cent rise in sales overall. At the end of the year, when sales bonuses were being calculated, they noticed that, as a result of the initiative, two sales reps were due bonuses in excess of £10,000. The Managing Director decided that the company could not justify these payments, and capped the commission at £6,000 for each rep. The two sales reps, who had been monitoring their sales performance throughout the year, were furious. They resigned shortly afterwards, and now work for another company.

This is an extreme case, when bonuses were capped retrospectively. However, even if you set a capped limit from the outset, it can be demotivating for a good sales person. You should use commission and bonus payments to encourage and motivate staff into working hard to reach their own ceiling, not an artificial one that you have created yourself.

So what constitutes a motivating performance bonus that will aid staff retention? It will vary between organizations, but somewhere between 10 per cent and 25 per cent of an employee's salary is a sufficiently high proportion to act as a serious incentive.

If you are looking for clarity and absolute fairness, an easy performance based system to introduce is a company-wide profit-related pay scheme. It is well documented that too many people do not differentiate between turnover and profit. A profit-related pay scheme will get every employee working towards profit, and is known to have a motivating effect. However, you will need to have an administrative system in place that can calculate profit on a weekly or monthly basis, unless you intend to leave profit related bonuses until the end of the financial year. There is a danger, though, that the motivational benefit will be lost if employees are in the dark about the organization's profit performance until the year end.

The profit-related bonus is just one of a number of types of bonus that you could establish.

Types of bonus scheme

We have already considered how a bonus scheme should, where possible, be linked directly with the overall business goals and objectives. There are few, if any, 'off the shelf' bonus systems that work for all organizations, so you will need to spend time considering a bonus system and structure that will work for you.

There are three broad categories of bonus scheme:

- bonuses that focus on the individual employee's performance or contribution
- bonuses that reward an individual team, department or division
- company-wide bonuses that reward all employees.

Let's have a look at each one in turn:

Individual bonuses

Piece work bonuses

With a piece work bonus, the employee is paid a basic wage (which may be quite low) and also a bonus related to their output. In a factory, for example, this may relate to the number of items produced. Bonuses of this sort tend not to have much of a motivating effect. They are considered more as 'sticks' for the company, rather than as 'carrots' for the staff. Piece work bonuses are usually established to keep the momentum of repetitive or mundane work going.

Commission

Commission-based bonus schemes are commonly used to reward salespeople. The salesperson is paid a basic wage, plus a commission based often on a percentage of the sales that he or she has made. Provided that the commission targets and levels are considered fair, many salespeople are motivated and engaged with this method of reward.

Individual performance-related pay

This involves rewarding an employee with a bonus payment for reaching specific targets set at the beginning of the trading year. It is generally considered that individual performance-related pay can be highly motivating for the individual employee, but can have a detrimental effect on the team or department that they work with.

Executive bonus schemes

These bonuses tend to be paid to key employees only. Targets are established for department or organizational growth and/or profitability. If these targets are met, then the key employee is rewarded with a bonus payment at the end of the period. Targets are usually challenging, but the bonus payment is substantial if it is reached.

Team or department bonuses

Although rewarding team performance is motivating for the employees involved, friction often arises between stronger and weaker members of the team. Inevitably, the stronger team members feel that they are being held back by the weaker ones. Some organizations manage this by offering an element of individual performance bonus as well as the team or department bonus.

Team performance

All the employees in a team or department share performance targets, and must work together as a team to achieve them. This might relate to manufacturing output (for example, number of products made), to service levels (percentage of calls answered) or to sales performance (number of products sold). These bonuses can be highly motivating, and can create a bond between team members. It is essential, though, that team members are able to monitor their progress towards the goals they have been set.

Project bonuses

With these schemes, projects are often broken down into key sections with milestones. A bonus payment is then made on reaching a key milestone, or on the successful completion of the project.

Company-wide bonuses

These are bonus schemes that reward all employees of an organization. A share of the end-of-period profits are distributed to employees, at a rate normally related to salary and/or length of service. These bonuses may be cash payments, or increasingly in the form of shares (under the New All Employee Share Plan).

Benefits of bonus schemes

There are a number of compelling reasons for introducing bonus schemes into your organization:

- they can relate specifically to company profitability, rather than turnover
- you can set targets related to specific areas that require improvement
- bonus payments can help an organization to recruit, motivate and retain staff
- they encourage employees by demonstrating that the organization is aware of their contribution
- they can give employees a greater understanding of the financial performance of the organization, particularly with regard to its profitability
- they provide important evidence of an employee or team that is working particularly well or badly
- they are a good way to build and promote teams.

Nevertheless, it is not always straightforward to introduce bonus schemes, and they do have some important disadvantages. Firstly, it is not always possible to link performance targets with an individual employee. For example, what performance targets can you set a secretary or personal assistant? He or she may well provide an essential role, but you may find it difficult to express the role in terms of personal, motivating targets that are linked to the overall business objectives. Or take the case of someone whose role is to research new plant machinery. What bonus scheme could you devise for them? If you plan to introduce individual bonuses for all of your employees, you will find it easier to set meaningful targets for some employees than for others.

Secondly, it is common for employees to become obsessed with their bonuses, and base every decision they make on the basis of its effect on their end-of-year bonus. For employees with roles that require some creativity or decision making, you would not want them to be so single-minded.

Thirdly, as we have considered earlier in the chapter, bonuses can create demotivated staff if there is a disagreement about how, and under what circumstances the bonus will be calculated and paid. So you must ensure that whatever bonus scheme you introduce, it is both fair and transparent.

Retention bonuses

You almost certainly know of organizations that reward the key milestones of long service. Examples include:

- a gold watch or clock for fifty years' service to a company
- one extra day's holiday or paid leave each year for each year of service given after five years – in other words, an employee who has been with the organization fifteen years is rewarded with an extra ten days paid holiday each year.

These long service awards tend not to have any retention effect. No employee would set out to stay with a company for fifty years, just because they needed a new clock. Some organizations, however, are beginning to reward retained staff after a much shorter timescale. For example, an organization may pay a bonus to employees after they have been with the organization for 12 months, and another one after three years. The principle is a simple one. By providing financial incentives, they expect to influence and persuade employees to stay. There are a number of problems with this approach:

1 It is indiscriminate. It rewards retained employees regardless of their motivation, enthusiasm, or even the quality of their work.
2 Research has shown that whilst financial incentives can play a part in the retention strategy, they are unlikely, on their own, to persuade a dissatisfied or demotivated employee to stay with an organization.
3 It can cause resentment and reduce morale unless all employees are included in the scheme, regardless of their role or length of service. If everybody is included, the rewards will quickly be regarded as salary, and any motivational or retention effect will be lost.
4 Rewards are divorced from the financial performance of the company.

The only genuine case for retention bonuses might be for short-term projects, for which suitably skilled employees are scarce.

You would not want to have to recruit new staff during the course of the project, and so you might offer a retention reward for employees who completed the term of the project.

Checklist

✓ Do you know how your salaries compare with other organizations in your business sector?

✓ Do you pay the 'going rate' or the 'staying rate'?

✓ Do you reward good performance with bonus or commission payments?

✓ Which employees could be paid and rewarded in a more motivating way?

✓ What bonus scheme might incentivize your employees?

✓ Do you give bonuses for individual, team or company wide performance?

employee benefits

In this chapter you will learn:

- **about the range of employee benefits you might offer**
- **about the merits of introducing a flexible benefits scheme**

Increasingly, organizations are looking at a wide range of benefits to offer to both new and existing employees. With employers fighting ever harder to retain their key staff, the skill required is to provide a package of benefits that meets the needs of individual employees. At the same time, employees are looking more closely at their futures. This chapter looks at the broad categories of benefits that are available to employers, and assesses how each might work in your organization. The chapter also considers the merits of a flexible benefits scheme, and how increasing numbers of organizations are adopting them.

Types of benefits

In the past, the salary that an employer offered was what motivated and retained staff. Today, employers and employees are much more flexible and inventive about putting together salary and benefits packages that are tailored to individual employees. So what are some of the benefits that you can offer employees?

Pensions

There are currently more than ten million people who are members of company or occupational pension schemes in the UK today. Although there is no legal obligation to set up your own scheme, a decent pension can be a valuable tool when attracting new employees to your organization and retaining the employees you already have.

In recent years, pensions have had a poor press. The value of many company pensions are based on the performance of the stock market. Since this has taken a big fall, the return on the employee's pension contribution has fallen with it.

There have been a number of changes to pension legislation in recent years. Stakeholder pensions have been introduced, and the State Earnings Related Pension Scheme (SERPS) has been replaced by the State Second Pension. There are several options to consider if you plan to make a pension part of your employee benefits package. These include:

- final salary schemes
- money purchase schemes
- group personal pensions
- stakeholder pensions

You will need professional advice about which type of pension might work best for your organization. You could contact the Society of Pension Consultants who will be able to put you in touch with a qualified adviser. Their phone number is 020 7353 1688. Alternatively, you can find further information about the types of pension available from the Inland Revenue website. Go to **www.inlandrevenue.gov.uk**.

Company cars

Until recent years, offering an employee a company car was a very attractive perk that enhanced a salary package considerably. A company car implied status, and employees made career decisions based on the make and model of company car on offer. Taxation has changed the situation. The executive saloon car is punished by heavy taxation, and employers are increasingly looking at the alternatives.

Like many employers, you could offer employees a cash allowance as an alternative to a company car, and then pay them a fixed mileage rate for using their own car on company business. This can be attractive, both to the employer and the employee. You may even wish to help employees to finance their car through a Personal Contract Plan (PCP), which is a lease or lease purchase agreement that may include the costs of servicing and insuring the car. This can work especially well for employees who have to visit clients regularly. Without assistance with funding, employees may purchase a cheap or unreliable car, which does not reflect the organization's culture. By offering a funding scheme, you can influence the choice of make, model and age of vehicle purchased.

Car parking

Providing an employee with a parking space at work can be a valuable tax-free benefit. However, there is a lot of discussion at the moment about whether to tax company car parking spaces, and you should consider the implications of such a tax before offering the benefit to an employee.

Meals

Could you offer free or subsidized lunches to employees? Meals are not taxed as benefits as long as they are made available to all staff. Providing all employees with luncheon vouchers, particularly if your organization is based in an expensive part of town, can be a popular benefit.

Loans

Could you offer employees personal loans? If you lend an employee up to £5000, the sum is not taxable and does not attract National Insurance. The most common form of loan offered is a season ticket loan. The employee borrows the money to purchase an annual season ticket loan at the start of the year, and then pays the money back, out of salary, over the course of the year.

You could use a similar scheme to offer personal loans to pay off bank and credit card debt. Such a scheme can build loyalty amongst employees, with the additional advantage of tying the employee to your organization for at least the duration of the loan.

Long service awards

Some organizations offer long service awards. These are not taxable provided that the employee has worked for the organization for at least twenty years. You can pay up to £50 for each year of service.

Parties

Annual parties and celebrations, paid for by the employer, are also tax free up to £150 per head. Although most organizations host some sort of Christmas party, it is still a perk or benefit that contributes towards the overall motivation of the workforce.

Professional membership subscriptions

If there is a relevant professional body, society or institution, you can provide membership for your employees. The employee does not incur tax on the value of the membership.

Discounts

If you are a retailer, could you offer a staff discount for the products or services that you sell? Staff discounts are not taxed and are often seen as a motivating additional benefit.

Mobile phones

How about offering employees mobile phones? This could work particularly well for employees who have to make business calls from home, and would otherwise need the cost of calls reimbursed. Since 2000, the cost of mobile phones, and any line rental and calls paid for by the employer, are exempt from tax.

Accommodation

With the cost of housing rising faster than ever before, job location is becoming an increasingly important factor for both recruitment and retention. Perhaps you have staff for whom it would be appropriate to offer free or subsidized living accommodation? For certain roles where the jobholder needs to live on the premises, like caretakers, living accommodation is tax free. For most other roles, living accommodation is taxed as a benefit. However, employees may not mind about the tax implications, and be glad to have accommodation that they are not paying rent or a mortgage for.

Healthcare

Increasingly, employees are looking for benefits such as healthcare and pensions as part of their overall package. Free or subsidized healthcare, provided by organizations such as BUPA or PPP, are taxed as a benefit, but are nevertheless regarded as attractive additions to a salary package.

Sports facilities

Providing sports facilities for your employees provides a strong incentive. External sports club subscriptions are extremely expensive, and many employees would make use of sports facilities if provided. The employee does not usually incur tax on the benefit, provided that the sports facilities are not made available to the general public. Offering membership of a public gym or sports club is a valuable and motivating benefit that many employees would value, but it is treated as such by the Inland Revenue and taxed accordingly.

Mortgage subsidy

Banks and other financial institutions often provide discounted mortgages and other financially beneficial products and services for their employees. There is normally a tax liability for the employee, but he or she is usually better off regardless. However, interest rates are particularly low at the time of writing, and incentives based on low interest rates for loans and mortgages are not the incentive they once were.

Childcare

As an employer, you can provide tax-free childcare facilities on or off the work premises. Your childcare facilities must be approved by the local authority, and you must make the facilities available to the children of all employees, whether male or female, part-time or full-time, to avoid an accusation of discrimination. Providing an incentive of this sort normally makes financial sense only for large organizations. As a smaller organization, you can provide your staff with childcare vouchers, but these are treated as an employment benefit by the Inland Revenue and taxed accordingly.

Non-statutory maternity leave

Providing your employees with maternity leave and pay in excess of the legal requirement has a strong retention effect. You could offer:

- longer periods of maternity pay
- longer periods of maternity leave
- fixed payment on return to work
- stepped working hours on return to work
- maternity pay at the employee's full rate.

Many organizations offer extended maternity leave and facilities, and this is regarded as a strong motivator by most employees. Furthermore, organizations are increasingly considering the issue of paternity. Although new legislation makes unpaid paternity leave mandatory if requested, many organizations provide both extended and paid paternity leave.

Other benefits

There are hundreds of other benefits, large and small, which are regarded as valuable by employees, and which can enhance motivation and retention in your organization. Some examples include:

- sabbaticals, gap years and secondments
- travel insurance
- time off in return for working late
- subsidized holiday accommodation
- time off for voluntary work
- free access to/provision of computers for home or personal use
- regular team days out.

Flexible benefits

Most organizations offer a range of benefits to their employees, in addition to their basic salary package. We have already considered the variety of additional benefits that an employer might offer, including:

- company car
- private health insurance
- contributory or non-contributory pension
- additional holiday entitlement
- favourable maternity and paternity pay and leave.

A growing number of organizations are recognizing that employees have differing needs and requirements, and are putting the choice of additional benefits in their hands. In effect, the employee designs his or her ideal remuneration package. The employer offers a basic salary, as well as an additional sum that can be spent on one or more additional benefits.

In practice, flexible benefits serve employees' individual needs, and are very motivating. If it suits the employee, he or she can take the additional sum in the form of a contributory pension. For employees with families, perhaps comprehensive health cover for the whole family would be a more enticing benefit? New employees may prefer a season ticket loan, or a discount on rail travel. Younger employees with few family ties may prefer a company car. Many employees, young or old, may be more incentivized by additional holiday allowance.

If you think that flexible benefits could give your organization a real advantage in terms of staff motivation and retention, you will probably need some professional advice. When establishing such a system, it is usual to begin by considering all the extra benefits that you could offer your employees, together with a 'value' attached to each one. This gives the employee a menu of benefits from which to select. As the employee's personal circumstances change over time, they can change their chosen benefits accordingly.

Flexible benefit programmes are in their infancy. However, increasing numbers of organizations are moving to take a more flexible approach to the benefits that they offer to their staff. Flexible benefits are likely to provide a significant advantage for organizations, with noticeable improvements in recruitment, motivation and retention, but employers should factor in the cost of establishing and administrating a flexible benefits scheme. Furthermore, they need to monitor the effect on retention, and evaluate the impact that flexible benefits are having on the organization on a regular basis.

Checklist

✓ What benefits do you currently offer to your employees?
✓ What additional benefits might you offer?
✓ Would a flexible benefits scheme work for your organization?

12 share ownership

In this chapter you will learn:

- **about the types of share schemes you could introduce**
- **the effects of shares on motivation and retention**

Research in the UK and USA has demonstrated that offering employees shares in the company can result in significant rises in motivation, productivity, performance and profit. Increasingly, employees are attracted by the idea of being shareholders, and offering shares and share options can attract staff to a company. There are an estimated 5000 companies offering share ownership schemes of one sort or another in the UK. This chapter considers the links between shares and retention, and summarizes some of the more popular share ownership schemes in operation.

Traditionally, offering an employee shares in the company had serious tax implications:

- the employee would have to pay income tax on the value of the shares
- the company would pay National Insurance contributions on the value of the shares.

However, successive governments have understood the retention incentive of share options, and have introduced methods to enable employers to offer shares to employees without burdening them with a tax demand that they are not able to meet. There are approved methods for rewarding either all employees in the company, or for rewarding key employees at the company's discretion.

Save-As-You-Earn (SAYE) Share Option Scheme

This is a savings plan linked to the option of buying shares at the end of a fixed savings period:

- Shares can only be purchased from the matured savings plan (usually three or five years).
- The employer grants the employee share options related to the total amount that they have agreed to save.
- There is a monthly savings maximum of £250.
- At the end of the fixed savings period, a tax-free bonus is payable (of up to about 5 per cent interest).
- The employee may then recover the savings and bonus, or use all or part of the amount to purchase shares.

The employee must pay Capital Gains Tax on any increase between the price at which they were offered shares, and the value of the shares when exercised.

The Save-As-You-Earn (SAYE) Share Option Scheme must be offered to all employees, on equal terms. This is not a scheme that you could use to incentivize key employees only. However, this is a scheme designed to incentivize and motivate all employees, and as such is likely to have a positive and beneficial effect on retention.

Share Incentive Plan (SIP)

Share Incentive Plans (SIPs) are designed to allow all employees to participate in their business and to encourage long-term shareholding by them. Introduced in the Finance Act 2000, the Share Incentive Plan (SIP) provides four types of share provision:

- **Free shares:** as the employer, you can make free shares available to employees, up to a limit of £3000 in a single tax year.
- **Partnership shares:** employees may purchase shares up to £125 per month out of salary (or 10 per cent of overall salary, whichever is lower). There is a minimum monthly contribution of £10.
- **Matching shares:** you can match your employees' purchase of partnership shares if you choose to. You can contribute no more than two matching shares for each partnership share purchased.
- **Dividend shares:** employees are allowed to re-invest dividends tax free, up to £1500 per year where appropriate.

As their employer, you can award shares for reaching certain performance or profit-related targets, which may increase their motivational effect further.

If employees retain their shares for at least five years, then there are no taxes payable. The employee may incur a Capital Gains Tax liability when they come to sell their shares. Usually an employee must forfeit their shares if they leave the company before the share options mature.

Enterprise Management Incentives (EMI)

EMI was established through the Finance Act 2000 with the specific intention of helping small companies to attract, retain and reward high-calibre staff. EMI applies to independent companies with gross assets of less than £30 million. In such companies, employers can reward a maximum of 15 key employees by offering tax-advantaged share options worth up to £100,000 each at the time the award is made.

In principal, these share options are straightforward to administer:

1 A date is agreed upon which the shares may be exercised (usually after at least three years).
2 At the time that the shares options are granted, an exercise price is agreed.
3 On or after the exercise date, the employee may purchase shares at the exercise price. The employee can sell those shares immediately, or within a further fixed period.
4 The employee is liable for Capital Gains Tax on the gain made.

What are the benefits of EMI?

If you offer your employees a potential stake in the company, you can expect retention and motivation of these employees to be enhanced. In comparison with paying extra salary to the employee, providing share options will not directly cost you any money. You will not normally have to pay an National Insurance Contributions (NICs) when the options are granted or exercised, or when the employee sells the shares. Furthermore, the costs incurred setting up the share option plans are tax deductible.

Points to consider

There are a number of issues to consider in deciding whether EMI is suitable for your company:

Does the company qualify?

EMI was introduced by the government to help small, higher-risk companies to recruit and retain employees with the skills that will help them grow and succeed. The company must therefore:

- exist wholly for the purpose of carrying on one or more 'qualifying trades'
- have gross assets of no more than £30 million
- not be under the control of another company (so if there is a group of companies, the employee must be given an option over shares in the holding company).

The main trades excluded from being qualifying trades are asset-supported trades such as:

- property development
- operating or managing hotels
- farming or market gardening.

Which employees are eligible and who should be issued options?

An employee cannot be granted options if they control more than 30 per cent of the ordinary share capital of the company. They must spend at least 25 hours a week working for the company or the group, or if the working hours are shorter, at least 75 per cent of their total working time must be spent as an employee of the company or group.

Subject to the above restrictions, an employer is free to decide which employees should be offered options. The sole test is that options are offered for commercial reasons in order to recruit or retain an employee.

What type of shares will be issued?

EMI provides some flexibility for employers. For example, it is possible to limit voting rights, or set other conditions in respect of shares which will be acquired on exercise of an EMI option. The shares must, however, be fully paid ordinary shares so that employees have a right to share in the profits of the company.

When will the rights to exercise options arise?

The options must be capable of being exercised within ten years of the date of grant, but there does not have to be a fixed date.

Examples of circumstances in which the options could be exercised include:

- fixed period
- profitability target or performance conditions are met
- takeover of company
- sale of company
- flotation of company on a stock market.

Options can be made to lapse if, for example, the employee leaves the organization.

Company Share Option Plan (CSOP)

This plan was originally introduced in the Finance Act 1984, with the intention of motivating and rewarding senior managers. As their employer, you grant a key employee the right to buy a fixed number of shares, at a fixed price, within a fixed period of time.

No employee may hold share options worth more than £30,000 at any one time. At the end of the fixed period, the key employee may purchase shares at the price fixed at the start of the contract.

As with some other share ownership schemes, you can impose certain conditions on the employee that must be met before he or she can exercise their options. These conditions might relate to turnover or profit targets that the employee must reach.

Since the Company Share Option Plan (CSOP) is designed to increase motivation and retention, you can ensure that an employee's options lapse if they leave the company before the date when they may be exercised.

Like other share ownership schemes, the employee is liable for Capital Gains Tax on the gain made when selling shares.

Benefits of share ownership

We have already considered the retention effect of offering employees shares in the company. The increasing numbers of Inland Revenue approved share ownership schemes testify to their ability to motivate and retain staff.

There are benefits for both you, as the employer, and for your employees:

Employee benefits

- They encourage employees to gain an understanding of the financial performance of the company.
- Shares provide employees with a stake in the future growth of the company. You are allowing and encouraging employees to benefit from the success to which they are contributing.

- You are providing employees with a potential financial benefit that does not cost them anything.

Employer benefits

- Shares are proven to be effective for recruitment and retention.
- Shares encourage staff loyalty.
- Shares give you the ability to reward staff with additional benefits without increasing salary, and without tying up valuable cash flow.
- Shares encourage your employees to think of the company's financial performance in terms of profitability.

There are some disadvantages, however. What if the value of the company falls during the period before options may be exercised? It can be demotivating for employees to discover that their share options are worth less than were forecast, or in the worst cases nothing at all. In addition, you should not discount the costs of administration associated with share ownership schemes.

Occasionally, the retention effect of a share ownership scheme can backfire. Consider the scenario of a relationship with a key employee breaking down, for whatever reason. The employee may feel obliged to remain with the organization, solely because they have share options in the company that they are not yet able to exercise.

Nevertheless, if you are looking for a positive step you can take to motivate and retain your key employees, offering a share ownership scheme may provide exactly the incentive required.

Establishing a share ownership scheme

If you are considering establishing a share ownership scheme in your company, you should seek professional advice. Before doing so, you might find the following checklist useful:

- What type of share scheme do you think might work best for you?
- Do you want to create immediate shareholders, or introduce a share option scheme?
- Are other organizations in your sector offering share incentives to their employees?

- Do you want to offer share incentives to all your employees, or just your key employees?
- Do you plan to link share options to individual or team performance targets?
- Are there other conditions that you might want to impose?
- Have you considered the tax implications of offering share incentives?
- Who will handle the administration involved?
- How will you advertise and promote the scheme within your company?

If you have thought about these issues, you should be able to provide a professional adviser with enough information to guide you effectively.

Further information

As with all elements of company legislation, the tax incentives and laws relating to share ownership change over time. There are plans, for example, for a new accounting standard that will require companies to show the cost of employee share schemes as an expense in their accounts. A professional adviser can help you to interpret these, and other changes to legislation, as well as advise about what changes you need to make with your share ownership scheme.

There are other sources of information regarding share ownership schemes. ProShare is an independent not-for-profit organization that promotes responsible share ownership. You can visit their website at **www.proshare.org**.

The Inland Revenue also provides information and advice about employee share ownership. Their website is at **www.inlandrevenue.gov.uk**.

Checklist

✓ Do you currently offer shares or share option incentives to any of your employees?

✓ How would introducing a share incentive scheme benefit your organization?

✓ Do you want to offer shares to all your staff or just your key employees?

✓ Where will you go for advice and further information?

13 motivation

In this chapter you will learn:

- **about a range of methods that organizations use to motivate their employees**
- **how to provide job satisfaction and role enrichment**
- **how to set motivating goals and targets**
- **how to build individual and team performance**

What is motivation? What steps can you take to motivate your key employees? Virtually all of the retention strategies outlined in this book will have a motivational effect. This chapter looks at the link between motivation and retention, and considers specific areas of your organization that are known to motivate or de-motivate employees.

Virtually all the retention strategies outlined in the chapters of this book will, in themselves, have a positive and beneficial effect on the motivation of your workforce. For a complete review of ways to motivate staff, you should consider:

- **Robust recruitment procedures (Chapter 7):** if you recruit the wrong people for the role or organization, you will find it very hard to motivate them.
- **Induction, training and development (Chapters 8–11):** training and development is regarded as a very important factor in how long an employee remains with an organization, and how motivated he or she is likely to be.
- **Salary, targets, bonuses and benefits (Chapters 12–14):** employees are motivated by a combination of salary and benefits that should be tailored to individual needs.
- **Creating a work/life balance (Chapter 20):** it is hard to be motivated if you spend too much time at or give too much commitment to work. Employees need to allow time for other interests outside the office.

Having said that, motivation and retention are not the same. There are countless methods for motivating your staff that you can introduce to your organization at any time.

Avoiding the 'them and us' syndrome

It is still common to see organizations with a 'them and us' attitude. In other words, there is a distance, either real or perceived, between the 'ordinary' workers and the management. Of more concern still, there are too many managers in organizations who are renowned for criticizing and punishing *poor* work, rather than recognizing and rewarding *good* work. It is not difficult to appreciate which approach is likely to motivate your staff. Criticism and punishment always causes staff to be demotivated. If you have any managers who are sparing with praise, and lavish with criticism, then what measures can you take?

Blame

One common symptom of many organizations is a culture of *blame*. Your mission should be to rid any team, department or even the whole organization of blame. Blaming someone or something else for mistakes that you make is like an infectious disease. You may even have the disease yourself. Try to ensure that the people for whom you are personally responsible recognize that mistakes are inevitable, and that they are things to learn from.

Help

Encourage your staff to ask for *help* when they need it, and to ask questions when they don't understand something. You may already know organizations where asking a question is regarded as a sign of weakness. Make sure your staff do not work with the same negative frame of mind.

Interest

Take an *interest* in your staff. Do you know what they do outside work? What hobbies do they have? What sports do they play? How did they spend last weekend, for example? What would your staff say about you? Would they say that you show an interest in them? Or that you are distant and withdrawn?

Team spirit

Develop a genuine *team spirit* with your staff. Do you hold daily, weekly or even monthly meetings with them? How do you ensure that every member of your team is working towards common objectives? You can use regular meetings to establish goals, to fill each other in on what you are doing, and to plan tasks and projects. You can also use them to swap news, to share problems and to praise good performance.

Partners

Treat your staff like *partners*. Ask your staff for their opinions before decisions have to be made. Keep staff informed about decisions that will affect the way the organization runs, as well as about company and team performance.

Goals, targets and objectives

It sounds like common sense, but no employee is motivated if they do not know what is expected of them. You should establish clear, unambiguous goals for your staff that reflect the objectives of your team, your department and, ultimately, of your organization, for example:

The principle should be that every employee understands where they fit into the organization, and how their role contributes to the overall business objectives. If they have a grasp of these two points, they are likely to be motivated to succeed. We have already considered goals and targets in relation to training and development (Chapters 7–9) and with regard to bonus and commission payments (Chapter 10).

Praise and criticism

It is alarmingly common to hear about managers who are ready to criticize when things go wrong, or when an employee performs badly, but are not so ready to praise when things go well. The effect on the employee can be extremely demotivating. From their perspective, performing well appears to go unrecognized, whilst less than excellent performance is brought to their attention speedily. So what are the rules to follow about praising and criticizing employees?

- Do it quickly: whether good or bad, it is vital to respond with your feedback as soon after the event as practical. Do not store up your criticism for an appraisal meeting, by which time you may lose your temper.

- Never personal: never criticize the person. Be critical of the consequences of an action, rather than the character or personality of the person who performed the action.
- Remember why: criticisms are designed to change behaviour to produce better results next time. So make sure that your criticisms are constructive, and that employees can learn lessons from them.
- Maintain a balance: it is much easier to criticize than to praise. It is easy to take the view that good performance should be the norm, rather than something exceptional. For good motivation, you must be as ready to praise as to criticize. You may have to make a conscious effort to praise good performance the first few times, if the experience is new to you, but it will become instinctive over time.

Job enrichment

Even your most loyal and enthusiastic employees may find their jobs mundane and unchallenging from time to time. An employee may voice his or her dissatisfaction in terms of the:

- amount of control that they have in their job
- level of responsibility they are given for their work
- lack of variety in their role
- challenge that their role provides
- lack of opportunity to use the skills that they have.

As well as these common causes of dissatisfaction, there are three main types of problems that employees face with the role that they perform:

Ambiguity of the role

If any or all of an employee's role is unclear or ambiguous, the employee is likely to be demotivated. Do your key employees understand the principle objectives of their role? Is there any part of their role that they may find unclear?

Conflict within the role

This is actually quite a common cause of demotivation. An employee may have two or more conflicting objectives. For example, a senior sales person may be charged with wining and dining corporate clients, selling to them face-to-face, but they may also have a key objective to cut costs and personal expenses.

Overload of responsibilities

If you give one of your key employees too many tasks to perform, or too many objectives to reach, they are likely to achieve very few of them. Their quality of work may suffer, and they may become disenchanted both with their role and with the organization as a whole.

As an employer, your role is to recognize a dissatisfied employee, whether they tell you about it or not. You should be prepared to stretch and challenge your employees when appropriate, and to reduce workload and priorities when necessary. You can also introduce variety into an employee's role, or give them an internal organizational role to perform, in order to keep motivation levels high. There are a number of steps that you can take:

1. Give your employee new tasks in order to create variety and diversity.
2. Give more responsibility to an employee who you believe can handle it.
3. Consider rotating repetitive tasks and jobs amongst staff.
4. Provide more complex tasks and roles for employees who need to be stretched.
5. Provide team-based tasks from time to time for employees who usually work alone.
6. Provide solo tasks for team-based workers occasionally.
7. Give an employee responsibility for a complete project, rather than just a part of it.
8. Be prepared to review employee roles frequently, and redesign them according to the skills invested in the employee, and the needs of the organization.
9. Ensure that you make use of particular skills that your employees have. It can be demotivating for an employee to have a skill or aptitude that is under-utilized by the organization.
10. If willing or appropriate, be prepared to move employees to a new site, department or team. Employees can become jaded working for long periods of time with the same team of people or in the same department.

Any one of these measures can enrich an employee's working experience, and can provide momentum, motivation and enthusiasm to remain with your organization.

Dealing with ambition

Learning how to recognize, fuel and manage individual ambition is a key management skill, and one which is beyond the scope of this book. Nevertheless, you may be able to differentiate between various employee types:

1 Employees who have ambitions in line with their experience and prospects, and that you want to retain in the organization for as long as possible.

2 Employees who want to 'run before they can walk'. They seem to have ambitions far beyond their skills or experience. They may be worth retaining, if only you could encourage them to have realistic aspirations.

3 Employees who seem to have little or no ambition. If they enjoy their job, and are effective at it, then these employees may well be worth retaining. If they appear demotivated, perform poorly, and have little ambition, then some form of intervention is required.

Recognizing an individual employee's ambition is part of the journey towards being able to do something about it. Most employers will admit to losing staff who moved on to a better paid, more senior role elsewhere. The employer was unable to offer a role or position that kept pace with their ambition.

Less common, but just as important, are employers who promote and create career paths for employees who neither want them, nor are ready for them, as the case below illustrates:

Case study

Steve works in a high street building society branch as a customer adviser. After a few months in the role, the position of financial adviser became available. Instead of being based in a branch, the financial adviser travelled to customers' homes and workplaces, and offered face-to-face advice about personal financial matters. Steve's manager assumed that he would be interested, and encouraged him to apply for the position. Steve's manager interpreted his protestations as expressions of modesty. After two interviews, the personnel department offered Steve the role. Steve thought that he had little alternative but to accept it. Besides, the extra money and the car would be useful. However, Steve hated the position. He felt inadequate for the role. He did not enjoy travelling, and he didn't really need the extra money. He had enjoyed the security that the branch-based job had offered him. After three weeks, he resigned. Fortunately, the personnel department had not been able to recruit someone suitable for the branch job, and so were able to offer Steve his old position. If they had not done so, they would have lost a skilled and competent branch adviser, albeit one with only modest ambitions.

As the story illustrates, providing new challenges and opportunities is not always the right approach to take. You need to consider what motivates and drives employees on an individual basis.

Providing opportunity

What steps can you take to ensure that you provide career development opportunities for your key employees? There are only so many opportunities for promotion that any organization can provide. Not every organization is able to offer a structured career programme, from when an employee is appointed to a junior position, through to senior management level. You have to accept that some employees will want to develop at a pace that you cannot keep up with. Nevertheless, employees who see future opportunities with your organization are more likely to stay. Here are seven measures to consider:

1 Use the performance review or appraisal system to talk to staff about their individual aspirations. What do they want now and in the future? Where do they see themselves in 12 months' time? Help them to set personal goals and targets that they will find motivating. You will find some clear guidance about performance reviews and appraisals in Chapter 8.
2 Promote from within the organization whenever you can. Internal promotions always improve motivation and morale.
3 Where you are unable to offer a vertical promotion, consider offering a sideways move for an employee who needs a new challenge.
4 Find other ways to challenge and motivate employees. Why not put together a team of key employees who together will manage special projects?
5 If appropriate, see if you can identify a structured career path through your organization. This may enable you to recruit higher calibre staff to junior positions because of the long-term prospects that come with the job.

6 Consider separately how to deal with employees who have specific skills or talents that are not being exploited by the organization. Think of ways to use those talents. Invest in training and development for all staff. Try to identify training opportunities and the needs of employees who are ready for a new challenge or promotion.
7 Conduct regular audits of skills to identify the talent that is already invested in the organization, as well as the skills and experience required to fulfil the business objectives.

The working environment

What sort of environment do you work in? What does it say about your organization? The working environment often reflects the culture of an organization, and can itself create or stifle motivation. So what can you change about your offices or workplace that might improve your employee's motivation?

Open plan

The traditional workplace, with offices for managers and senior staff, often does little to promote communication or motivation. By contrast, open plan offices tend to be more effective for teams and departments because they promote discussion and communication amongst staff.

Relaxation

Do you give your staff anywhere to sit down and relax, away from their desks? Providing leisure space can be a very effective way to build relationships amongst employees. It can also offer somewhere to sit and be creative.

Facilities

Is it practical for you to offer sports facilities, or other leisure activities at your workplace? Could you provide a shower for staff who cycle in to work? What about lockers to store cycling kit?

Is your workplace kitchen well stocked? Is it a popular place to be, or do your staff drink coffee at the nearest coffee shop? What about a microwave? A big fridge?

The facilities that you provide may make all the difference between a motivated and a demotivated employee.

Team-building events and activities

Some people love them, whilst others hate them with a passion. Whatever your view, team-building exercises and activities can build effective teams fast, and employees who work well together as a team are usually highly motivated. You will need professional advice about what sort of activity or exercise would work best for your organization. There will always be staff who are not keen, but it is worth seeing it through, as the following case study illustrates:

Case study

One well-known company chose to send all its managers on an outdoor training and development weekend. There were videos and presentations, as well as assault courses and role-play exercises. Before the event, many of the managers were extremely cynical about the worth of the event, and resentful at having to give up half a weekend. However, many of the assault course activities taught fundamental lessons about working in teams and choosing a leader. The activities clearly identified certain types of manager: the one who barks orders, the one who would much rather let someone else decide what to do, the one who dominates the activity and wants to take part in everything, etc. Eighteen months on, the managers of this organization still talk about the weekend. Even the most cynical will admit to having learned a great deal, and having had a lot of fun!

Communication

To what extent do you promote communication in your organization? It is well established that poor communication is one of the most common complaints that employees make about the organization that they work for. But it is not just communication between workers and managers. It transcends the whole organization. If you think that communication is poor in your organization, what can you do about it?

Team meetings

Teams and departments should be meeting regularly to set objectives, to review progress and to celebrate success. Unless project timescales are particularly long, meeting at least once a week is essential.

E-mail

We know of organizations where e-mail has almost replaced speech entirely. For example, in some organizations, if an employee is thinking about making a round of tea, they e-mail their colleagues to inform them, and invite them to place orders. This may be an extreme example, but many of us are guilty of relying on e-mail too heavily. E-mail is a vital, and wonderful communication tool, but it should be used appropriately. Encourage your staff to talk to each other!

Strategy

If you introduce many of the training and development steps considered in Chapters 9–11, you will create an environment where every member of staff understands their role in the organization and how it contributes towards the overall business objectives. If you set individual profit- or performance-related bonuses (see Chapter 12) then you will inevitably encourage your employees to take more interest and involvement in the organization's overall performance and profitability. It is motivating to share with your staff the business plan, financial performance and company goals and objectives.

Variety

Make use of all the communication channels at your disposal. Use the company Intranet. Communicate by notice board, newsletters, face-to-face, e-mail, and so on.

Ask for help

Staff are motivated if they believe that their manager listens to them, and that the organization is interested in their opinion. Whenever you can, take the opportunity to share ideas with your employees. Ask for their opinion (before making a decision), and be prepared to change your mind if a good argument is made for an alternative proposal. You may wish to create a staff forum, where employees can put their ideas forward for consideration.

Top to bottom

Good communication is essential for the whole organization, right up to the chairperson or managing director. We know of several organizations where staff are motivated because the most senior people are visible, accessible and prepared to discuss their ideas and proposals with their staff.

Culture

If it is firmly embedded, there is not a lot you can do to change your organization's culture. However, if you are aware that the organization is considered a bit stuffy and old fashioned, for example, then perhaps it is time to think creatively! Is the perception justified? Take a look around you. If you were coming into the organization for the first time, what impression would you have? Have you noticed that some key employees have left to work for a new or recent competitor? What is their organizational culture like? What impression comes across from their offices, their advertisements, their staff?

If you suspect that the culture of your organization may be contributing to higher than average staff turnover, then maybe it is time to act!

Awards and winners

In this chapter, and the last, we have looked at various ways you might motivate by setting goals and targets for your key employees, and then rewarding them when they are reached. Many employers take a more public view, and spread news of successful achievements around the entire organization. Some examples include:

- employee of the month
- salesperson of the month
- customer service representative of the month
- employee who answered the most customer service calls
- most improved employee of the month
- employee with highest number of orders processed.

Most people like public recognition for their efforts, and enjoy celebrating success. You could follow the example of companies who frame the monthly awards in a reception area or public part of the workplace. In addition, some companies offer a prize, bonus or incentive to accompany the award. A monthly achievement award might be:

- £100 in cash (although this will need to be declared and taxed)

- lifestyle activity day (hot air ballooning, a day at a health spa, etc.)
- shopping vouchers
- dinner for two
- weekend break
- high-value consumer items, such as televisions, DVDs or cameras.

If you are considering introducing regular achievement awards, there are a couple of rules to follow:

1 Think carefully about the basis on which the awards are made. You need to ensure that the same employees do not win the awards each month. Start the scoring mechanism afresh after each award is made. This will make sure that all employees begin each month with a clean slate.
2 Make sure that you create lots of winners. Winning is infectious and motivating.
3 Hand out awards frequently. Monthly awards are the most common.
4 Publish the results, or hand out the awards publicly. Use the company intranet, a newsletter, e-mail or a notice board to make public the names of the awards winners.

Would introducing monthly awards and incentives reflect the culture of your organization? If so, you may find that the motivating effect of winning becomes infectious, and awards of this sort could become an important part of your retention strategy.

Checklist

✓ How motivated are your key employees?
✓ What steps do you already take to motivate your staff?
✓ What new measures could you introduce?
✓ How do you and your managers handle praise and criticism?
✓ Do you provide sufficient opportunity for your employees?
✓ Do you do enough to enrich your key employees' jobs?
✓ Is communication an issue for you?
✓ How do you develop team spirit in your organization?
✓ What does the workplace environment say about your company?
✓ Could you introduce an awards and winners programme effectively?

part four

retention costs and effects

consequences

In this chapter you will learn:

- **that some staff turnover is beneficial**
- **how limited staff turnover can provide opportunity for others**
- **how very high retention should not be your goal**

It may not be obvious, but having a high staff retention rate is not always a good thing. There are advantages and disadvantages associated with staff turnover, and the challenge organizations face is to find a balance between retaining all your employees and bringing in fresh blood. This chapter considers the advantages and disadvantages of staff turnover, and considers how to strike that balance.

Consequences of staff turnover

We have considered at length many of the reasons why staff turnover rates have been increasing constantly over the last twenty years. With employees feeling increasingly responsible for their own careers, it is considered normal to seek promotion through changing employer, rather than progressing within one organization. From the employer's perspective, it is worth repeating why retaining staff is so important. There are several clear benefits:

- Recruitment is expensive, and can be very time-consuming. The less often you need to recruit new staff, the more time and money you will save for your organization.
- Training and development is also costly and time-consuming. The more knowledge and skills that you can retain within the organization, the better.
- An experienced, retained workforce is likely to be more productive, and achieve better results.
- A constant workforce can deliver improved loyalty from your customers. On the whole, customers prefer to deal with individuals, rather than organizations. It gives them a sense of belonging. It can be off-putting to a customer to deal with a different person each time they contact the organization.

In addition to the benefits of retaining staff, there are many negative consequences of staff turnover:

- Staff turnover can cause significant disruption to those staff that remain. Projects and responsibilities may be left unfinished, with the expertise and experience required to complete them no longer available.
- Replacing staff at regular intervals often requires changes to the structure and make-up of teams and departments, and this can be demotivating. Most people find change difficult to handle, and high staff turnover can contribute to their anxiety.

- Losing expertise and experience through staff turnover is a problem, but it is more serious still if the expertise and experience has been lost to one of your competitors. Your ideas, working practices, and even your customers may move to your competitor along with your ex-employee.
- You may have certain staff with skills and expertise that are hard to come by. Losing these may provide a real problem because they will be hard to replace at any cost.
- Dissatisfied employees may trigger a wave of other resignations when they leave. Even if other staff are retained, levels of morale can be hit hard as a consequence.
- Staff may leave as a result of increased workload or pressure. By leaving, they increase the workload and pressure for those who remain. Again, this can have a detrimental effect on morale, and may lead to further resignations.

Opportunities presented by staff turnover

Having considered the reasons why staff retention is so important, it should be noted that there are positive consequences of staff turnover as well.

A staff resignation is an opportunity to look again at your staffing requirements. Here are two practical examples:

Case study 1

A direct marketing agency employed a part-time PA for one of the company directors. They also employed someone part-time in their sales team, whose role was to turn the salespeople's notes into well-presented proposals. The part-time PA resigned because she was getting married and moving to London. The agency recruited a replacement PA, also on a part-time basis. In fact, the part-time sales team member was looking for a full-time time position. He would have been interested in a full-role that encompassed both generating the proposals and working as a PA. If the agency had regarded their PA's resignation as an opportunity, they may have thought of this possibility themselves. Instead, the part-time sales team member also resigned shortly afterwards to move to a full-time position elsewhere.

Case study 2

A high street retailer of maps and travel books employed someone on the shop floor who was soon due for retirement. Before he left, the managers got together to consider his replacement. After a lengthy discussion, the managers concluded that the demand for paper maps was such that a full-time retail staff member could no longer be justified. However, the demand for digital maps was soaring, and staff in that department were fully stretched. So it was agreed that the retirement of this employee was a good opportunity to strengthen the digital maps department, and reduce the paper maps department by one.

These two examples show how important it is to use a resignation or retirement as an opportunity to look carefully at your current staffing needs. Perhaps you do not need to recruit after all? Or maybe you should recruit to a different position? You may find that you would be better off recruiting someone more senior, or more junior, than the outgoing job holder.

Staff turnover allows for restructuring of teams or departments. Although change can be demotivating for employees, staff turnover can provide the opportunity you need to make changes to the structure and make-up of teams and departments.

Staff turnover provides better promotion prospects for the staff that remain. Employees look for jobs with prospects. If staff turnover rates are especially low, it may seem to employees that the only way to progress their careers is by switching to an alternative employer. As a result, a manageable level of staff turnover can motivate other employees by creating new vacancies in key positions.

Staff turnover allows you to bring fresh blood into your organization. There is an argument that organizations increasingly need to 'think outside the box', and bringing in staff from outside provides an obvious method for looking at business issues from a different perspective.

Staff turnover can provide organizations with the opportunity to introduce more flexible working practices. Full-time leavers can be replaced by part-timers, flexitime staff, or job sharers. Salaried employees could be replaced with freelance or contract staff. With today's employees looking for greater flexibility, a staff resignation can provide you with the chance to think again about what sort of employee to recruit or promote.

Staff turnover may actually reduce your overall staffing costs. Since replacement staff are often less experienced than the leavers, you may be able to recruit a replacement at a lower salary.

Your mission is not to eliminate staff turnover altogether. You need fresh blood, as well as the opportunity to promote from within, and this is best achieved through a controlled turnover of staff. You should concentrate on putting as many measures in place that will retain your key staff:

- staff with skills and experience that are hard to come by
- staff with the greatest potential for the future (the rising stars)
- staff who best represent the culture of your organization
- staff who deliver the most profitability
- staff who your customers trust and respect

Checklist

✓ Has your staff turnover over recent months provided opportunities for others?

✓ Have you been able to bring fresh blood into your organization?

✓ What level of staff turnover would be beneficial for you?

✓ What steps can you take to strike a balance between retaining staff and maintaining a beneficial level of staff turnover?

15 the costs of retention

In this chapter you will learn:

- **how to identify the direct and indirect costs associated with retaining staff**
- **how to identify the direct and indirect costs associated with losing and replacing staff**

Retaining staff is an expensive business. This chapter looks at the obvious, as well as the hidden, costs associated with staff turnover. It compares these costs with the alternative costs of introducing measures to retain key employees. Although retention measures are expensive, many would argue that they constitute an investment, rather than an expense – an investment that will reward your organization handsomely in the years to come.

The costs of losing and replacing staff

Do you know how much staff turnover costs your organization each year? Consider the direct financial costs incurred when a single member of staff leaves:

Temporary replacement

Perhaps your employee left the organization straight away, without serving a notice period? If so, you may need to arrange temporary cover while you recruit a full-time replacement. Perhaps you will have to pay overtime to another member of staff to keep up with the outgoing employee's workload? If your recruitment drive does not offer up a suitable candidate, you may need to extend the period of temporary cover.

Severance

Under certain circumstances, you may require the employee to leave the organization, and you may incur some level of severance pay as a result.

Advertising

Recruitment advertising is expensive. If you need to advertise in local or national newspapers, professional or trade journals, or with an online recruitment agency, you will need a significant budget to do so.

Agency costs

If you plan to use the services of a recruitment agency or headhunter, there are substantial costs to consider. You may have to factor in an extra 10–15 per cent of the new recruit's first year's salary in agency costs. If you are recruiting a senior member of staff, the costs may be higher still.

Interview and selection

Selection tests are best handled and interpreted by professionals, and their costs must be considered. You may need other professional help with the recruitment process. You ought to reimburse the travel and other expenses incurred by each shortlisted candidate who you interview. You may have to pay for a medical examination for your first choice candidate.

Induction

Costs associated with induction include relocation expenses, where required. You may have to pay for temporary accommodation for your chosen candidate.

Training and development

You are unlikely to find a replacement member of staff with exactly the right skill set required for the role and for your organization. You may incur significant expense with initial training and development (although you may have been able to recruit your new member of staff at a lower salary as a result).

As well as the direct costs, there are several indirect, or hidden costs that you may not be able to measure:

- What impact has the staff resignation had on the business? Could sales have been affected as a result? For example, if the employee leaving was a salesperson, perhaps their territory has suffered a noticeable reduction in turnover since they left?
- Has the employee taken customers with him or her? Has the employee gone to a rival organization? What effect might this have on your own business performance?
- Has the staff resignation affected morale in other employees or teams? What disruption has the resignation caused to other members of the team or department involved?
- Has the service you offer to customers been affected? For example, if the employee leaving was a customer care person, have the levels of service dropped?
- How long did it take for the replacement employee to get up to full speed and capacity in the role?

Then there are the time costs associated with a member of staff leaving:

- manager's time to conduct exit interview
- line manager's time writing references for outgoing employee

- administration time dealing with payroll and employment documentation
- administrative time to write, organize and place recruitment advertisements
- the time required to meet and brief a recruitment agency effectively
- time for reading through applications, and making an initial shortlist for interview
- time for conducting preliminary interviews on the telephone
- time for interviewing (which may require several, senior members of staff for days at a time)
- time to shortlist again and conduct second interviews, if required
- time for selection
- time to administer the checking of references, the contract of employment, the offer of employment letter (as well as the time spent rejecting unsuccessful candidates)
- time to organize and manage the new employee's induction into the organization
- extra time spent managing and supervising your new recruit over the first few months of employment
- training and development time and effort.

If you express staff turnover in terms of direct, indirect and time-related costs, it is plain to see that staff turnover can cost an organization dearly.

Case study

A cut-price German supermarket chain entered the UK market in the early 1990s. They embarked on a programme of recruiting several dozen Store and District Managers in the Midlands and North of England. The company sent each District Manager on a training and development programme that included three months in Germany, working in German supermarkets. The trainee managers were put up in hotels, with every expense paid for by the company. On returning to the UK, the trainees were moved around the country, staying in hotels for a further six to eight months. Little expense was spared with getting the training and development right. One senior manager estimated that it cost the company at least £50,000 to train and develop a single District Manager (twice the initial annual salary). However, they expected huge returns, and many District Managers resigned within the first year of employment. At one stage, only two or three trainees out of ten actually fulfilled the role of District Manager for more than 12 months. Staff turnover significantly hampered their early success in the UK.

If you have suffered significant staff turnover over the last year or so, it might be worth putting an estimate to the overall cost to the organization. Try working through the list of costs opposite to establish a total annual cost for your turnover of staff.

Costing retention

In Chapter 14, we considered how some staff turnover is good for an organization. As an employer, staff resignations enable you to promote other employees, and also to bring in fresh blood. The goal is not to eliminate the costs of staff turnover altogether. Rather the target to set is to limit staff turnover to manageable proportions, whilst working hard to identify and retain your key employees. Retaining staff, however, also comes at a cost.

As with turnover, there are direct, indirect and time-related costs that need to be accounted for:

- the cost of providing key staff with benefits such as company cars, medical insurance, pension contributions, and so on
- bonus and commission payments and incentives
- training and development costs
- administrative costs involved with establishing and managing individual motivation and incentive programmes; managing personal development plans
- the cost of providing shares and share option schemes to all/key employees
- the extra staff costs to cover employees with extended holiday allowance, maternity leave, and so on
- the cost of team-building and other motivation events and activities
- the management time required to establish, manage and evaluate individual motivation and retention programmes.

However, not all the retention strategies outlined in this book are expensive. Establishing rigorous recruiting practices in order to find the right member of staff is only a little more expensive than poor recruitment practices that lead you to make the wrong choice. In fact, assuming the unsuitable recruit subsequently leaves the organization, then rigorous recruitment practices will cost you less.

A number of the most simple retention tactics are free:

- praising as well as criticizing
- telling others about good performance
- asking employees for their opinions
- involving and communicating with your staff
- crowning an 'employee of the month'.

Others only cost the organization in direct proportion to turnover or profit increases, or improved business performance:

- bonuses and commission
- awards for reaching specific sales targets
- salary increases.

Although all of these retention costs are important, many human resource professionals would recommend that you regard them instead as an investment. The improved retention, and reduced turnover, that results is your return on that investment.

In practice, you need to consider the wider viewpoint, establishing a balance between a number of issues:

1 Estimating an appropriate level of staff turnover that will bring business benefits to the organization
2 The costs of staff turnover within estimated levels
3 Staff turnover costs over and above estimated level
4 Specific costs associated with identifying and retaining key staff
5 Company-wide employee benefits and their estimated return on investment
6 Bonus and commission payments, balanced by a related increase in turnover or profit

Introducing specific retention strategies may require from the organization a substantial investment of both time and money. If, however, the strategy is linked to specific retention and staff turnover target levels, you can expect to make considerable cost savings associated with recruitment and selection. In addition, the improved motivation and effectiveness in your key employees should provide a handsome reward on the investment made.

Checklist

✓ Do you know what staff turnover has cost your organization this year?

✓ Could you estimate the impact that staff turnover has had on sales, on customers and on other employees?

✓ Have you estimated what all the retention measures that you have introduced have cost this year?

16 the work/life balance

In this chapter you will learn:

- **about the needs of different employee types**
- **about flexible working methods**
- **about family-friendly policies**
- **about the importance of creating the work/life balance**

The way we work is changing all the time. Increasingly, people have to contend with responsibilities both at home and at work. More and more lifestyle managers are promoting the need to be creative, and the benefits arising from a work/life balance. But what does this actually mean in practical terms? What can you do to facilitate an improved work/life balance in your organization? This chapter considers the implications of the work/life balance for employers, the business benefits and the legal obligations.

In Chapter 2, we considered the many ways in which the nature and make-up of the workforce is changing:

- a higher percentage of the workforce is female
- there is an increasing number of families where both partners go out to work
- there are increasing numbers of women returning to work after having a baby
- there are larger numbers of people with responsibility for the care of elderly relatives.

Is it any wonder that there is a strong movement towards improving the work/life balance? At times, most employees find that work demands get in the way of their non-work and other commitments. For example, managers and professionals often need to take work home at the end of the day. In a recent survey by the Chartered Institute of Personnel and Development (CIPD), just 33 per cent of workers acknowledged that their employer had any family-friendly practices or personal support services in place.

Family-friendly practices

The principal movement towards family-friendly practices has begun, inevitably, with childcare. Increasingly, women are returning to work after having a baby, and problems arise with arranging childcare and support, school journeys, school holidays, after-school care and meal preparation. Although the focus of childcare support has been on women, men benefit from family-friendly policies as well.

Other needs

It is not only employees with families who have care responsibilities outside work. There are increasing numbers of workers with responsibility for the care of elderly or disabled friends and family. Other workers may have no immediate dependants, but have other commitments within their local community. We have seen how more and more employees are taking responsibility for their own careers, and so these employees need time to study for further skills and qualifications. With more emphasis on promoting a healthy lifestyle, other workers are looking for time and opportunity for sports and leisure activities outside work.

In fact, just about everybody has a stake in the work/life balance debate, and everybody stands to benefit from it.

The business perspective

Research has indicated that employees who spend too much time at work, and have a poor work/life balance, will suffer many symptoms over time. These include ill health, poor morale, absenteeism, a lack of commitment, and a tendancy to make mistakes at work.

By contrast, organizations who adopt family-friendly and flexible working policies can expect a number of business benefits. These include:

- improved motivation and retention
- increased commitment from employees
- applications from higher calibre candidates when recruiting
- applications from wider range of applicants
- improved productivity
- more flexibility to staff busy periods (like lunch hours) and to provide cover (during staff absence and holidays)
- creation of a more informal, open and trusting working culture
- reduced overheads for accommodation, IT, furniture and other equipment.

So there is a strong business case for creating a working environment that respects the employees' desire to have a better work/life balance. Although you may face additional costs in adopting more flexible policies, the costs are usually outweighed by the gains.

Having looked at the business case for adopting flexible working practices to improve the work/life balance, it is time to consider the specific measures that you can take.

Flexible working patterns

The first step you can take is to look at the way that you currently expect your employees to work. The majority of organizations still employ staff on the basis of a fixed working day. In too many companies, there is a culture of working long hours. The specified working day may be 9 a.m. to 5.30 p.m., but in reality employees feel under pressure to work longer hours. Their performance, they would argue, is not based on what they achieve, but on how many hours they remain at work.

This is changing. With the work/life balance higher on the employee's agenda, employers need to offer more flexible working arrangements. These include:

Part-time working

Part-time work is the most common form of flexibility offered to employees. If you contract any member of staff to work fewer than basic, full-time hours, you are effectively employing a part-time worker. Part-time work is very useful to people who have care responsibilities, or who have other demands on their time. However, more and more senior professional staff are switching to part-time positions, happy to take a reduced salary in return for more free time. Even younger employees with portfolio careers are increasingly moving towards two or more part-time positions in preference to a single, full-time job.

Part-time work may suit ideally a woman returning to work after having a baby. She may not want to continue to work full-time. Could you split the responsibilities of their role up so that you can offer them a part-time position?

Flexitime

As its name suggests, flexitime allows workers to be more flexible about which hours they work. Often an employee with a flexitime contract must work a set number of hours each week or month, but can specify, within reason, when to start and finish work each day. Flexitime works well for staff with childcare commitments, because they can deliver children to nursery or school before coming in to work. By offering flexible working terms, you may well retain the services of a new parent. Flexitime also works increasingly well with our hectic schedules today. Staff can take a morning off to wait for a plumber, for example, or they can start later each day in order to benefit from a reduced commuting cost. In the public sector, as many as four out of five employers offer flexitime, compared with only one in four in the private sector.

Staggered hours

Employers increasingly use staggered hours in order to keep organizations staffed over an extended period. If you offer workers different start, finish and lunch-break times, you can maintain sufficient staffing levels over the whole working day.

Job sharing

Job sharing is when two people share responsibility for a role, or for achieving certain objectives. The two employees are jointly answerable to their line manager, and often work on separate days to combine to make up a full-time position. In the UK, it is becoming more common to offer positions to job sharers, and employers are starting to recognize the many advantages that they bring to an organization.

Employers often complain that they lose good employees because their circumstances change such that they are no longer able to work full-time. If the demands of the role dictate that it would not suit a part-time employee, then the employer often loses a good member of staff. Job sharing can provide the answer.

Term-time working

Term-time workers may be employed on a permanent contract, but are able to take either paid or unpaid leave during school holidays. This type of work is of great value to employees with young children. They may be able to work full-time during term time, but cannot arrange cover or support for their children during extended school holiday periods. Not every job suits a term-time working contract, but by employing term-time only workers, you may open your organization to a range of talent that would otherwise be unavailable to you.

Time off in lieu (TOIL)

Time off in lieu allows employees to take time off to compensate for extra hours worked. Formal and informal TOIL arrangements have existed for a number of years, but their value has increased recently. Employees are increasingly willing to put in the extra hours when required, as long as they can claw back this extra time during quieter periods.

Compressed hours

A compressed hours worker delivers the same number of hours during the working week as a full-time worker, but covers them over fewer days. So they may work from 8.00am to 6.00pm Monday to Thursday, rather then 9.00am to 5.00pm Monday to Friday.

This type of arrangement can work well for workers with a specific outside commitment on a particular day of the week. For example, they may need to visit relatives in care, go to college, or play sport for a local club. Some workers prefer compressed working week contracts so that they can regularly enjoy a long weekend.

Annual hours

Annual hours contracts enable a worker's hours to be calculated over a full 12-month period, rather than over a working week or month. This is not a common way to employ staff, and is mainly used in specific industries where this type of flexibility works for both the employee and the employer.

Shift working

Shift working has been standard practice in the manufacturing sector for decades. It is usually only relevant in organizations that need to be staffed 24 hours a day. Over recent years, shift work has become increasingly common in the retail sector, with many stores extending their opening hours into evenings and weekends. The major supermarket chains all now offer a number of 24-hour superstores.

Home working and teleworking

With the rapid advance in technology, the push to improve congestion and pollution by working from home is finally gaining momentum. In the past, employers have felt unable to manage staff effectively unless they were based at the organization's premises. Their lack of confidence has many causes:

- insufficient accountability
- inability to assign and manage workload
- lack of trust
- uncertainty about precisely how the worker from home spends his or her time.

Evidence has suggested, however, that employees who are entrusted to work from home are actually more productive and time-effective than their office-based colleagues. There are countless examples of organizations who employ a range of staff on a full-time and part-time basis from home. With fast Internet and network access, working from home can deliver an immediate and marked improvement on an employee's work/life balance. It is particularly suitable for:

- workers with families – for example, a parent with a young child may only be able to work in the office from 10 a.m., having delivered their child to school and travelled to work. But they could start work at 9.15 a.m. if they were based at home
- other employees who can only commit to certain working hours
- certain types of workers, like bookkeepers and analysers
- employees whose commute to work is particularly awkward.

Zero hours contracts

Zero hours contracts are offered to employees who work only when they are needed. This is a common form of employment in pubs, restaurants and clubs, where staff are needed to cover busy periods.

Extended leave of absence/sabbatical

In some organizations, the employer allows or encourages a worker to take an extended break, either paid or unpaid. It is particularly common in the education system, where teachers and lecturers may take leave to travel, research, or write a book or journal. There are a number of examples where unpaid leave has led to increased motivation and improved staff retention, as the following case illustrates:

Case study

Stanfords is the world's largest map and travel book shop, with UK branches in London, Manchester and Bristol. Because of its specialist service, it has tended to employ young staff who are experienced travellers. On the positive side, the company can provide customers with passionate and experienced help with their travel requirements. On the negative side, staff were often demotivated because they were itching to go travelling again, rather than working in the retail sector. The management decided to tackle this issue by offering unpaid leave to all staff once they had been with the organization for three or more years. Stanfords has seen many of its staff take leave to travel, and then return to the company to save for the next trip. Customers have benefited from ever more experienced staff, and motivation and retention levels have increased well above the industry average.

Legislation

There have been a number of changes to employment legislation over the past two years, specifically designed to increase employees' rights with regard to flexible working. If you are in any doubt about the extent to which your organization complies with the relevant legislation, you should seek professional help. However, you may find the following summary useful:

Annual leave

All employees are entitled to a minimum of 20 days paid annual leave.

Working week

The working week is limited to 48 hours. This is calculated as an average over a 17-week period.

Parental leave

New legislation provides both men and women with a right to up to 13 weeks unpaid leave at any time up to the child's fifth birthday. The employee must take this in blocks of at least a week at a time, with at least 21 days' notice given to the employer.

Dependant care

Employees have a right to take time off, unpaid, to deal with a family emergency, concerning a family member who is living with them.

Maternity leave

From April 2003, mothers are entitled to 26 weeks' maternity leave, with an additional 26 weeks' available for certain employees.

Paternity leave

From April 2003, fathers are entitled to two weeks' paternity leave.

Part-time workers

Part-time employees are entitled to the same rate of pay as a full-time worker on a pro rata basis. They are also entitled to the same holiday and paid leave allowance, also on a pro-rata basis. Part-time employees must also receive the same rights to contractual sick pay.

Flexible working request

From April 2003, employees with children (aged six years or younger) can request a change in their working hours, time or place of work. The legislation also applies to parents of disabled children up to the age of 18. The employer may refuse the request, but must consider it seriously, discuss the request with the employee, and detail the reasons for the refusal in writing. A refusal may be made on a number of grounds:

- the recruitment costs of providing additional cover
- the organization's inability to meet customer demand
- the level of work available at the times that the employee wishes to work

• the impact the change will have on team performance or quality.

Further details about this new legislation are available from the Department of Trade and Industry website. Go to **www.dti.gov.uk**.

Although you are legally entitled to refuse a flexible working request, you should think hard before doing so. Your employee is likely to leave as a result. You should balance their needs and yours before coming to a decision.

As well as making sure that your organization complies with recent legislation, you should also ensure that your flexibility policy does not discriminate in any way. You will find a short guide to discrimination in the Appendix.

Although the legality of your approach to flexibility is important, it is more important still to consider how you can meet your employee's needs whilst maintaining your focus on the needs and objectives of the business. The work/life balance issue is not going to go away. It is building momentum all the time. Working with employees to improve their work/life balance will be a critical success factor for retaining key employees in the future. You may prefer to think about it now.

Work/life balance action plan

When developing a strategy for improving your employees' work/life balance, the first step you can take is to talk to the employees themselves. What is their view about time at work and time outside work? What are their motivators? What groups of needs do you need to address? How do your employees perceive the issue?

Before committing to any changes, you also need to look at the issue from the perspective of the business. What are the needs of the business? What impact will the changes you might introduce have on these business needs? How will having a work/life strategy benefit the business, and the workforce, as a whole? Consider the impact on all the stakeholders: How will customers benefit? How will shareholders benefit? How will employees benefit?

Having considered the issues, you are in a position to develop some clear guidelines. What policies are fair? Which requests from employees are unattainable? Over what time period will you introduce the new strategy?

Try and involve employees throughout the development process. Make sure that you have your managers and colleagues on your side (sometimes managers are wary of introducing flexible working arrangements because of the perceived increase in management effort required). Always ensure that you conduct a small pilot for any flexible working initiative that you introduce, and that you evaluate its impact afterwards.

Checklist

✓ To what extent do you consider the needs of your employees?
✓ What family-friendly policies do you offer/could you introduce?
✓ How would your organization react to a request for flexible working patterns?
✓ What can you do to help your key employees to achieve their own work/life balance?

17 retention in practice

In this chapter you will learn:

- about the practical application of retention strategies for different types of employee
- how staff retention requires a personalized approach
- what different types of employee look for from you

In the last chapter we considered the drive towards an optimum work/life balance for all employees. This chapter looks at how to use flexible working incentives in conjunction with a range of other incentives and benefits.

We all have different motivators. An incentive or benefit that motivates one employee, may cause another to leave the organization. In this chapter, we consider the various motivations and needs of your different employee types, and how you can design a retention package for each.

You are unlikely to find a flexible working option, or a single package of benefits that will satisfy all your employees. There is not one overarching strategy that will solve your turnover problems at once. We all have different needs, ambitions and motivators, and we are constantly changing. It is almost necessary to devise a separate retention strategy for each individual employee.

Your different employee needs

Take a brief look at your staff. Consider, for a moment, how they vary in terms of their:

- gender
- age
- skills levels and experience
- life stage
- ambition
- length of service
- length of time in the industry
- level of responsibility.

Having an understanding of the types of people that you employ may help you to identify what matters to them most. If you understand what people want from their job, then you are likely to be able to offer them what they are looking for.

Employees with families

Parents of young children have to juggle a number of commitments and roles outside work. They must deliver children to school or nursery, provide meals, look after them when they are sick, attend school functions, and so on. It is common for an employee's values, drive and commitment to change dramatically once they become a parent. Their new responsibilities mean that they are not able to be as flexible as they once were. You may know of an employee for whom their job was the most important thing in their life, until they became a parent.

So what specific measures can you take that will increase your chances of retaining staff with family commitments?

Nursery provision

Some organizations, usually larger ones, have a crèche or nursery on site. Others provide financial support towards the cost of childcare provision. This can be a key factor for staff on maternity leave when considering whether or not to return to work. Could you subsidize or provide childcare support for your employees?

Career breaks

Do you often find that employees do not return from maternity leave? Why might this be? Are you sufficiently flexible in what you are able to offer those returning to work?

Maternity leave

The level and extent of maternity support that you provide may influence how well you manage to retain mothers returning to work. Organizations increasingly offer extended maternity leave and additional maternity pay. Paternity leave and pay is becoming more common. Coping with becoming a parent can be incredibly stressful, and any additional support that an organization can provide is likely to be rewarded with retained and motivated staff.

School holidays

School holidays can be particularly difficult for parents to manage. Children need to be supervised and entertained for extended periods. Some organizations offer holiday play schemes or additional leave during school holidays. Holiday periods are a real concern for parents at work, so any support from your organization may have a positive effect on retention.

Flexible hours

We considered in Chapter 16 the importance of part-time, flexitime and other flexible working methods for employees with young familes.

All of these family-friendly practices will have a beneficial effect on:

- motivation
- retention
- job satisfaction
- absenteeism
- work quality.

Case study

Katie was keen to return to work soon after having her first baby. Her employer was worried that she would not want or be able to handle the workload and pressure that her job involved. In fact, what mattered most to Katie was finding appropriate and affordable childcare provision. Katie had lost none of her drive and ambition, but would have welcomed some help in the form of a subsidized nursery or childminder.

Young employees

Young people often have very different demands and expectations of a job. If they have been to college or university, they may have debts that need to be paid back as quickly as possible. Some will want to save for a home, so that they can join the spiralling property ladder as early as they can. Others will be glad to be young, free and single, and have few needs other than to earn sufficient money to keep up with their social life.

If you can identify the particular needs of your younger staff, you will be in a better position to devise a retention strategy that will work for the employees that you believe can contribute to the business objectives on a long-term basis.

You may find that younger staff, new graduates and school leavers will be most switched on by:

- short-term rewards and bonuses
- clearly defined goals and targets
- few administrative duties.

Tip

Remember that people's needs and motivations change as they get older, or as their lives change as they get married, have a baby, etc. A single member of staff may love the motivation of a target-driven, commission-based sales position. He or she may enjoy the independence of being out on the road visiting customers, staying away from home during the week. But the situation may change completely if their personal circumstances change. With a family, the employee may find the pressure of commission-based pay hard to cope with. Staying away from home may be a problem. As their employer, you need to recognize how people's needs change over time, and devise a package of benefits to suit their individual circumstances if you want to retain them.

Older employees

Older employees may be looking for stability. They have worked though an age when they will have witnessed countless friends and colleagues being made redundant, who then find it hard to find new work in their forties and fifties. They may even have been in that situation themselves. They are more likely to value:

- longer-term benefits and rewards
- share options or long-term bonuses
- pensions or retirement benefits.

However, the option of flexible or part-time working may appeal to older workers, giving them more time to follow other pursuits, or even to semi-retire. Other older workers will still be looking for a new challenge, so you should think about other roles you might offer them:

1 Could they teach or run internal training courses?
2 Could they take on a coaching or mentoring role?
3 Could they take on new projects or commitments?

You need to consider the stage that each employee is at. If you can identify what drives each of your employees, then you are likely to be able to devise an appropriate retention strategy for them.

Graduates

Newly graduated staff are often looking for particular challenges and opportunities:

- They may be looking for ways to rise quickly through the organization, and may find routine or repetitive tasks boring. You need to be able to provide guided career development for the graduates you recruit and employ. Or perhaps you do not need to recruit graduate calibre staff? If you are unable to provide the development opportunities for graduates, you are unlikely to keep them in the organization for very long.
- Graduates will be looking for formal and informal training and development opportunities. Can you provide them?
- A new or recent graduate may want to acquire broad work experience quickly. You may be able to retain graduates by offering them a range of roles and responsibilities, or you may lose them because they can broaden their experience by switching employer.
- Increasingly, graduates look for high levels of reward for the effort they put in. They may have student debt to pay back, and highly incentivized pay may provide just the motivation a graduate is looking for.
- New or recent graduates may have fewer commitment or family ties. They may be more flexible than other staff in their working time and patterns. They may be happy to travel, to move location, or even work abroad more readily than other employees.

Usually you can expect to retain a new or recent graduate for up to about two years. Statistics show that a graduate is likely to seek a new opportunity within a two-year period of graduating. You will need to provide both challenges and development opportunities to retain the services of a recent graduate beyond two years.

Managers and directors

Managers and directors of the organization are often forgotten in the drive to retain staff. It is often assumed that their seniority alone provides the challenge and opportunity needed to keep them in the organization. In fact, managers and directors have needs and demands as important as any other group.

- Managers may be looking for a longer-term commitment from you. They may be at a stage when they either need to find new employment, or commit to the organization long-term. Loyalty bonuses and incentives such as share options or retention bonuses may be ideal.
- Managers may be looking for a new challenge. What could you offer within your organization? It is dangerous to assume that staff at management and director level are motivated and challenged by what they do.
- Can you make use of their skills and experience in other ways? Could they take on a training or development role?
- Managers and directors may well be family people, and as such may value highly opportunities to work more flexibly. Perhaps they could work from home for some or all of the time? Perhaps they could work flexible hours, or part-time?
- Employees at this level may think more carefully about exactly what they want to achieve. Perhaps there is something that they have always wanted to do, but have never had the opportunity, like travelling around the world. Offering a sabbatical or career break may provide just the incentive needed to retain the services of a manager or director for the long term.

Retention flexibility

It is not just the work/life balance that demands flexibility. As we have seen, there is not one, single retention strategy that will appeal to all of your employees. What motivates an experienced manager will hold no appeal to a new or recent graduate. Offering financial support with childcare is of no consequence to a long-service worker with no family. Indeed, providing such opportunity can cause resentment in those for whom the benefit does not apply, as this case study illustrates:

Case study

The owner of a small direct marketing agency realized that many of his employees had young families with children of school age. He was sympathetic to requests from employees to start work early, and leave early, so they could collect children from school. After a round of performance appraisals, it was agreed to introduce this flexible working policy formally. Many of the employees with families were delighted, and greatly appreciated the increased flexibility. However, it was vital to maintain sufficient staff coverage across the whole day, and so younger staff with no family were encouraged to work later, and were discouraged from working on earlier shifts. The situation worsened when staff with families were given preference for taking time off during school holidays. The resentment increased in those employees who did not have children. What was meant to be a motivating and retention driven exercise caused greater turnover of staff for whom the benefits did not apply.

This case demonstrates that you need to consider a wide range of opportunity and benefits in order to retain staff, and your retention strategy must be fair and equal at all times. Furthermore, you must never reward or incentivize one group of staff at the expense of another. More importantly, your retention strategy must avoid challenges of discrimination (see the following Appendix).

In summary, you may need to consider a different package of benefits and opportunities for each employee, or employee group:

- flexible working hours, shifts and patterns
- extended annual leave
- maternity leave and career breaks
- fast-track training and development
- support with childcare
- new challenges and opportunities
- share options and long-service rewards
- short-term incentives and rewards
- long-term incentives and rewards.

Checklist

✓ Do you know the benefits that each of your employees would value highest?

✓ Do you have staff with young families? What could you offer them that will retain their services for the foreseeable future?

✓ Do you employ graduates or young staff? What are they looking for from their employer?

✓ What strategies can you adopt to retain senior managers and directors?

✓ How flexible can you be with your retention strategy?

appendix: discrimination

You have a duty at all times to ensure that your recruitment and retention procedures are fair, legal and anti-discriminatory.

There are four main areas of discrimination covered by legislation: equal pay; sexual discrimination; racial discrimination; disability. There is a wealth of legislation protecting both employers and employees, and in almost all cases it is preferable to take professional legal advice when establishing new retention initiatives, rather than take a risk.

We list below the main acts concerned with discrimination, along with sources where you can get more detailed help and guidance.

Equal Pay Act 1970

The Equal Pay Act (1970) makes it unlawful for employers to discriminate between men and women in terms of their contracts of employment. You need to be aware that it covers all the contractual benefits, not just pay. So there must be equality in relation to:

- holiday entitlement
- pension
- childcare benefits
- sickness benefits
- car and travel allowances.

There are two excellent sources of further information:

- Equal Opportunities Commission
  www.eoc.org.uk
  They publish a Code of Practice on Equal Pay which gives practical advice and guidance on discrimination, as well as case studies illustrating examples of discrimination on the basis of equality.
- Equality Direct
  www.equalitydirect.org.uk
  A free service affiliated to ACAS that gives business managers easy access to authoritative advice on a wide range of equality issues. The website has sensible advice and guidance written in plain English, whilst further advice is available for the price of a local phone call.

Sex Discrimination Act 1975

The Sex Discrimination Act makes it unlawful for an employer to discriminate because of a person's sex or marital status. Every part of the recruitment and employment process is covered by the Act including:

- job descriptions
- person specifications
- recruitment advertisements
- application forms
- shortlisting procedures
- interviews
- selection methods.

Further help

The Equal Opportunities Commission publishes a Code of Practice on Sex Discrimination, which gives guidance to employers and employment agencies on measures that can be taken to achieve equality between men and women. Further details are available from their website:

- Equal Opportunities Commission
  www.eoc.org.uk

Race Relations Act 1976/Race Relations Amendment Act 2000

The Race Relations Act 1976 and the Race Relations Amendment Act 2000 make it unlawful to discriminate on the grounds of race. Race can be defined in terms of:

- racial group
- colour
- nationality
- ethnic origin.

The Act applies to Great Britain only (England, Scotland and Wales). There is a separate Race Relations Order that applies to Northern Ireland. The Act covers all employers regardless of their size, and provides protection to all employees including vocational trainees and agency workers.

All aspects of the employment relationship are covered including:

- recruitment and selection
- promotion
- transfer
- training and development
- pay and benefits
- redundancy
- dismissal
- terms and conditions.

The Act includes provision for direct and indirect discrimination, as well as victimization. You can find practical, up-to-date information about the Act from the Commission For Racial Equality website.

The Race Relations Amendment Act 2000 came into force on 2 April 2001. It requires public authorities to have due regard to:

- eliminate racial discrimination
- promote equality of opportunity and good relations between people of different racial groups.

With regard to recruitment and retention procedures, you should monitor the recruitment, selection and progression of ethnic minority staff (and students) by grade, type of contract, pay and other benefits.

Exceptions

There are a limited number of exceptions to the above legislation. These are when being of a particular sex or race can be regarded as a genuine occupational qualification (GOQ). Examples include:

- actors or dramatists playing a specific role
- overseas workers, where the laws of the country worked in prohibit certain races, or gender, from doing the work.

Further details of these exceptions are available from the Campaign For Racial Equality website:

- Commission for Racial Equality
  www.cre.gov.uk

Disability Discrimination Act 1995

The Disability Discrimination Act 1995 introduced new measures designed to end the discrimination which many disabled people face.

It protects disabled people in areas of:

- employment
- access to goods, facilities and services
- the management, buying or renting of land or property
- education.

Many of the Act's measures became law for employers in December 1996. Others are being phased in gradually.

With regard to recruitment and employment:

- It is unlawful to treat disabled people less favourably than other people for a reason related to their disability.
- Employers must make reasonable adjustments for disabled people, such as providing extra help or amending the job role.
- From 2004, employers may have to make reasonable adjustments to the physical features of their premises to overcome physical barriers to access. Obvious examples include ramps, lifts and other means to ease access.

Further information is available from the Disability Rights Commission. They publish an excellent Code of Practice, copies of which can be ordered by telephone, or downloaded from their website:

- Disability Rights Commission
  www.drc-gb.org

Some useful websites

www.personneltoday.com
The website for HR professionals

www.ipd.co.uk
Chartered Institute of Personnel and Development

www.businesslink.org
The National Business Advice Service

www.statistics.gov.uk
National Statistics Online, including national employment and training statistics

www.monster.co.uk
Currently one of the leading online recruitment websites

www.fish4jobs.co.uk
Currently one of the leading online recruitment websites

www.workthing.com
Currently one of the leading online recruitment websites

www.eoc.org.uk
Equal Opportunities Commission

www.equalitydirect.org.uk
Equality Direct

www.cre.gov.uk
Commission for Racial Equality

www.drc-gb.org
Disability Rights Commission

www.investorsinpeople.co.uk
The official website for Investors in People

www.inlandrevenue.gov.uk
For information about pensions, and the tax implications of bonuses and incentives

www.proshare.org
Independent, not for profit organization promoting responsible share ownership

www.mintel.co.uk
Market research analysts

www.statistics.gov.uk
The Office of National Statistics, who publish *Labour Market Trends*

Books

Recruitment and Selection: A Competency Approach (Developing Practice), Gareth Roberts, 1997, Chartered Institute of Personnel and Development

A Manager's Guide to Recruitment and Selection, Margaret Dale, 2003, Kogan Page

Competency-based Recruitment and Selection: A Practical Guide (Strategic Human Resource Management), Robert Wood and Tim Payne, John Wiley and Sons Ltd

Employee Recruitment and Retention Handbook, Diane Arthur, 2001, Amacom

Recruitment and Selection (Professional Manager), Financial Times Prentice Hall, 1999

Successful Graduate Recruitment, Jean Brading, 1998, Hawksmere Ltd

Readymade Job Advertisements: A Recruitment Toolkit for Every Manager, Neil Wenborn, 1991, Kogan Page

Principles and Practices of Recruitment Advertising, Bernard S. Hodes, 1982, Frederick Fell Publishers

The Difficult Hire: Seven Recruitment and Selection Principles for Hard to Fill Positions (Career Savvy Series), Dennis Doverspike and Rhonda C. Tuel, 2000, Impact Publications

50 One-minute Tips on Retaining Employees, David Hayes, 2001, Crisp Publications

Recruiting and Retaining People, Florence Stone, 2002, Capstone Publishing

Retaining Top Employees, J. Leslie McKeown, 2002, McGraw-Hill.

index